From Graveyard to Ambition
THE OFFICIAL HISTORY OF THE
SWANSEA CITY
SUPPORTERS' TRUST

From Graveyard to Ambition
THE OFFICIAL HISTORY OF THE
SWANSEA CITY
SUPPORTERS' TRUST

Phil Sumbler

Forewords by Huw Jenkins
& Kevin Johns MBE

AMBERLEY

This book is dedicated to the memory of Mike Kent and Richard Lillicrap – both stalwart believers in the supporters' trust movement and driving forces behind our organisation.

First published 2013

Amberley Publishing
The Hill, Stroud
Gloucestershire, GL5 4EP

www.amberley-books.com

British Library Cataloguing in Publication Data.
A catalogue record for this book is available from the British Library.

ISBN 978 1 4456 1939 2 (print)
ISBN 978 1 4456 1957 6 (ebook)

Typesetting and Origination by Amberley Publishing.
Printed in the UK.

Contents

Foreword by Huw Jenkins

Looking back ten years, it seems impossible to recognise the club as they are now. So much has changed since the club ownership changed in 2001, and thankfully most of it is for the better.

The story of Swansea City does grab attention and it is usually either myself or the supporters' trust that are mentioned highly when reporting that story, but we should never detract from the fact that we have a large number of people who were prepared to stand up and make a difference as we watched the club being ripped apart.

I have been fortunate to be the head of the club for the large part of our journey but there is no way that we could have succeeded without these people and, of course, this group includes the supporters' trust.

Firstly through Leigh Dineen, who is now my vice chairman, and now Huw Cooze, we have had two hard-working directors who have added great value to the club during their time on the board. Their roles are potentially different from some of the other shareholders as they are not representing their money but the money of the supporters, the lifeblood of any club.

I do believe that the model we have adopted at Swansea City is the right model, especially with the supporter ownership. That we are all supporters ourselves means that we have Huw there with his voice representing us all; it is important to make supporters feel part of the club and that their voices are heard.

I don't think any one of us will ever forget those days back in 2001 when everyone fought so hard to save the club. Thankfully, we did it, and look at everything that has happened since! To see this club in the Premier League and now in Europe should make everyone who played a part back then sit up now and feel proud of what we have achieved. We have a new stadium as well and sell it out week on week and are looking to expand it so that we can accommodate the demand and desire to watch us as a football club.

In the same vein that the club is held up as a role model, the trust are held up as a role model for a supporters' trust, and rightly so. They have been part of this journey from the beginning and they have worked tirelessly over the years to help make the club better for all of us. For any group of supporters, to raise the sums of money that they have to gain the stake in the club that they own is remarkable and I would never want to see that change. Their presence helps safeguard our future for the next generations of Swans fans and that is important.

I hope you enjoy their story and realise just what a part they have played, along with the rest of us.

Huw Jenkins
Chairman, Swansea City Football Club

Foreword by
Kevin Johns MBE

Everyone who has been involved in the Swansea City Supporters' Trust should be incredibly proud of the part that the trust has played in the success story that is Swansea City!

I don't suppose that anyone gave thought to the fact that the trust would still be a part of the club's life some thirteen years after its inception.

The early days were all about the 'then', about fighting the fires that raged and threatened to destroy what was, is and always will be the greatest football club in the world.

Things have changed at Swansea City Football Club and the activities of the trust have moved on, as has the club.

The early years were all about playing a part in the survival of the Swans, about raising money among those who would have given the shirt off their backs if it would have helped!

I will never forget the public launch of the Swansea City Supporters' Trust on a Bank Holiday Monday evening at the Patti Pavilion.

Any family members who had planned a Bank Holiday evening trip to the Mumbles for a Joes or sausage and chips at Dick Bartons were forced to forget those plans as hundreds of fans left the Vetch and headed for what was possibly one of the most important gatherings of Swans fans in the history of this great football club.

In the weeks and months ahead, Swansea City fans, far from feeling a sense of helplessness, found a voice in the trust and, while times often seemed very dark, the trust always provided light at the end of the tunnel!

In the early days, the trust helped raise money to support salaries and was able to secure shares in the club and a place on the board.

If Swansea City's success story can bring hope to the clubs in League One and Two and the Conference, then the Swansea City Supporters' Trust should be an example to fans of clubs in every league.

Over the years, the trust have continued to support the club where needed and have been a voice for every supporter, and long may it continue to be.

Some seasons ago the trust launched the Robbie James Swansea City Wall of Fame, which was unveiled at the Liberty Stadium, and over a period of five years the trust will induct twenty names per year at the annual Swansea City Player of the Year Awards.

When history looks back at the last dozen or so years in the history of this great club, it will undoubtedly record the huge role played by the Swansea City Supporters' Trust.

Kevin Johns MBE

Introduction

An Ugly, Lovely Town.

Dylan Thomas, 1914–53

There is probably little doubt that Swansea is the most idyllic location of any Premier League football club. Situated on the coast of South Wales, it is the gateway to the Gower Peninsula, which was the first area in the UK to be given the title of an 'Area of Outstanding Natural Beauty' in 1956.

It is home to some of the most outstanding beaches in the UK, one of which (Rhossili) was voted the third best in Europe in a 2013 survey. It is a city that is steeped in tradition, a city that recovered from extensive bombing in the Second World War, and a city that has since recovered to become what it is today.

Its football team was formed in 1912 and played their fixtures a little more than a long goal kick from Swansea Bay at the Vetch Field – their home for over ninety years, before a move to the Liberty Stadium in 2005.

During those 100 years, some of the best footballers ever produced in the British Isles have donned the white shirt of the Swans and played for a club who, in the main, have spent their time outside the top flight of English football. But the city has always been proud of the football club and has backed them in numbers over the years, only to see them fall short on so many occasions.

However, by the time the 1970s came around, the club was flirting with the bottom end of the Football League, and re-election (as it was back then) was applied for by the club for the very first time in the mid-1970s. There was brief respite in the late 1970s and early 1980s thanks to the arrival of Welsh legend John Toshack, but that was short-lived as the club rose to the top so quickly before falling down just as dramatically upon his departure.

Mismanagement was a word often used during the period that followed, as the club lurched from one disaster to another, with the occasional promotion followed all too soon by what seemed to be an inevitable relegation, and the bottom division looked to be a place that was destined to hold the name of Swansea City.

But all that changed a little over ten years ago, when the supporters decided enough was enough and stood up to fight for their football club. No longer were they to sit back and let people run their club into the ground – they were to make themselves heard, take the club by the scruff of the neck and make a difference.

This book tells the story of the Swansea City Supporters' Trust – a proud owner of more than 20 per cent of their football club. A collective body of supporters wanted to make an impact on a small corner of South West Wales, but it was a small corner that would bring them worldwide recognition and a place as a role model for how things can, and maybe should, be done in the football world.

This is a rags-to-riches tale and a remarkable story of how hard work, more than the odd stroke of luck, and the collective effort of supporters can achieve almost anything. It highlights that football fans do not have to accept what is placed in front of them, and that if a city can collectively stand behind its football club then any battle can be won if you fight together.

Dylan Thomas may have uttered the words at the start of this introduction and they may have been immortalised as something less family friendly in the film *Twin Town*, but Swansea is a success story and one that every football fan should be proud of.

Miracles Can Happen

Our greatest glory is not in never falling,
but in rising every time we fall.
Confucius, 550–478 BC

You may think that the use of the word 'miracle' is rather over dramatic, but I really cannot use any other word to describe what has happened at Swansea City in the last ten years. To rise from the bottom of the Football League to European football, and from a club that literally did not have two pennies to rub together to making multi-million-pound profits, in such a short duration is nothing short of miraculous at any time. But to achieve that in a period of football where money appears to be everything is even more incredible.

I was lucky enough to just be starting on my Swansea City supporting journey when John Toshack was here in the late 1970s and early 1980s, and I remember vividly our battles against the top-flight clubs in English football. I remember dreaming in 1982 that we could be crowned League champions, and I remember watching that dream turn into a nightmare as we slipped down the league divisions, almost losing our club in 1985.

I remember the pride I felt in 1994 as we graced the hallowed turf of Wembley and the pain just three years later as we were robbed of a play-off final win at the same ground, but those days were just brief respites in a rollercoaster ride that everyone will tell you is what watching the Swans is all about.

It was not long after that second visit to Wembley in 1997 that I found myself purchasing my first Windows PC, and from that moment on my time watching the Swans took on a whole new character. It was at that point that I found myself directed to a mailing list about the Swans called Swanmail, where I could read and share views on the Swans with fellow Jacks worldwide. And that, I believe, is a time that totally changed the way that we interacted with our football club, and how we viewed the day-to-day running of the club going forward.

I was an exiled Jack at this point in time, so the ability to be completely up to date with happenings at the Vetch was vital to me, and it was through this medium that I met a good friend of mine in Keith Haynes and the rest of the MAGS, who had their own avenue into the club as a recognised supporters' club.

It was also via this medium that I was introduced to the views of the likes of Leigh Dineen, Mike Kent and Richard Lillicrap, who were all people that had a vision and a dream of the development of a supporters' trust in Swansea. They were prepared to stand up and be counted, and many an email was exchanged via that forum between all the members on how a football club could be run as we headed towards the twenty-first century.

My involvement in the club went one step further when, in the summer of 2001, I was handed the reins to jackarmy.net, completely unaware that, within three months of being given my admin username and password, the face and future of the club was to change forever.

If I was being totally honest, when the trust was first set up for the Swans, I was a little sceptical about the motives of those who were behind it. I believed in the concept completely, as my joining the trust at the very outset proved, but I was not alone in believing that some were in it for their own personal gain rather than a desire to see an improvement of the football club for the benefit of all the supporters. However, as time went on and I watched the people involved giving up their time to fight for the football club – particularly during the ownership battle of 2001 – then my scepticism of the trust faded, and the website became more and more supportive of the workings of the trust and the need to succeed in its mission to preserve professional football in Swansea.

In 2005, a change of working circumstances meant I had more free time to myself and I stood for election to the trust board for the first time. I was fortunate to come through the procedure to take my place on the board, moving into the chairman position just twelve months later – a position that I still hold at this publication date.

Of course, it would be wrong to claim that all the changes are down to the trust, and we know of many people outside of the trust who have played a massive part in evolving the club to where we are now. All of the shareholders and directors have done their bit, but it is the story of the trust that tends to catch the eye and make people sit up and take notice.

Ever since the final whistle blew at Wembley to signal our entry into the Premier League on that magical day in May 2011, the perception of the trust, not just in Swansea but far further afield, changed beyond anything I think any of us expected. Media enquiries came in from across Europe and beyond as the world woke up and realised just what an incredible story that of Swansea City really was.

We had known it for several years. We had got used to the passing game that is 'The Swansea Way' and we knew the shrewd way that the club was being run by our chairman, who had grown into the role since he first took it on over ten years previously. What surprised us more was that we probably assumed others just realised what we were doing but chose to ignore it. But such is the reaction of the media to anything that sits outside the walls of the Premier League that we really were the best-kept secret in English football.

In the two years that have followed, it has been plaudit after plaudit for the club, but also for the trust, as we are hailed as a role model for any supporters' trust, and are lauded as an organisation that offers hope to any club in crisis. In the modern game, there are too many of them for my liking. I have also lost count of the number of trusts in the UK that have asked us for help, and just recently we have made presentations at meetings of supporters' trusts as we are held up by our governing body, Supporters Direct, as the perfect model of what a trust can achieve.

It is fair to say that had anyone suggested to me back in 2001, when I attended my first trust meeting at the Patti Pavilion, where we would be situated twelve years on, I would have laughed for many days and probably recommended medical help for the person that suggested it. We really are proof that anything is possible if you dare to believe, and to the visionaries that first discussed the idea of the trust back at the turn of the century, I thank you on behalf of Swansea fans everywhere for starting the ball rolling.

I hope that this book gives you some idea of the work that has gone into making Swansea City and the Swans Trust what they are today. At times you may feel that you are reading a short history of the last ten years of the Swans themselves, but it is fair to say that we have played a massive part in that history and I have tried to include a trust perspective, where possible from the people who were involved at that time.

I hope that you enjoy the book, and at this point I would like to dedicate it to two people I mentioned earlier, Richard Lillicrap and Mike Kent, both of whom had the passion to drive for a supporters' trust, although sadly neither is around to see the results of that passion come to fruition. This one is for you YJBs.

Enjoy the book.

Phil Sumbler
Chairman, Swansea City Supporters' Trust

1

The Beginnings

The killer application will not be a shrink-wrapped program
that sells in millions. The killer app will be a website that touches
millions of people and helps them to do what they want to do.
                                    Lou Gerstner, Chairman of IBM

It is difficult to pinpoint exactly when the idea of a supporters'
trust in Swansea first reared its head, but I do firmly believe that
the roots can be traced back to a series of meetings that were not
widely publicised. You may well question why meetings that did
not get publicised actually got any attendees, but they evolved
from a very humble beginning and developed into a passion for the
Swans that had probably not been seen outside the Vetch Field or
maybe some of the pubs around the area on a matchday.

These meetings did not take place in pubs or clubs but they
involved many hundreds of people, all of whom had their own
opinions of the Swans both on and off the pitch. And they involved
many people who cared passionately about our football club and
who desperately wanted it to succeed.

But, most bizarrely, they took place in complete silence with no
words actually being spoken. This was the evolution of the Internet
and the catalyst for many friendships and, for many, a completely
different view on the Swans and the club they all supported.

Prior to this point, for many the only insight into our football
club was through the production of fanzines which, in their own
style, gave the views of the writers to a wider population than just
thoughts in their own heads.

But while the printed fanzine had its place, it was the Internet that changed the way that many saw the football club and, more importantly in the evolution of the trust, it was the medium that changed the way that many viewed the action off the pitch rather than on it.

The Swans were in the hands of Silver Shield when I remember reading on the Internet the views of people who were vocal about the motives of our owners and who expressed their fears for the future of the football club. Ironically (but probably not surprisingly), some of these people are now heavily involved in the football club, which shows a great desire to not just speak through a medium such as the Internet, but to stand up and make a difference, something that has remained close to the heart of us as a supporters' trust since we launched.

The first introduction for many to Swansea City on the Internet was thanks to a schoolteacher from Llanelli, who used his skills to launch the popular website scfc.co.uk. While many sites have been spawned to cover the Swans over the years, this was the start, and with it Gary Martin also founded a mailing list that still exists to this day – Swanmail.

Over to Gary to explain:

Swanmail and scfc.co.uk were started because there was very little happening on the Internet about football clubs – especially for those outside of the Premiership. In those days, all the club sites were run by enthusiasts and Swansea were up there with Liverpool, Aston Villa, West Ham, etc., and the problems that webmasters were getting from the clubs were shared and discussed among the groups.

The hierarchy at the clubs saw this as some spotty teenagers working away in a back bedroom – although I didn't fall into this category! – and tried to dismiss it as the latest fad tat that would soon die out.

My motivation was manifold. First, as in all things, I wanted to do a professional job and do it well. Secondly, it was to connect with people from outside the area with up-to-date news on all things Swansea City. Thirdly, it was to help raise the profile of the club, though no recognition for this was sought or received.

I was surprised at how quickly a worldwide network sprung up via the site and a glance at old programmes from the time will feature articles I wrote highlighting some of these. One of the most satisfying episodes was the site being instrumental in getting a promising US teenager from Florida a trial with the club. Nothing actually came of it in the end, but it was an insight into the power of the Internet at those early stages.

I do remember one of the main movers in bringing a supporters' trust to Swansea was Richard Lillicrap – he was genuinely committed to the idea from the start and it was his persistence that I am certain helped achieve this.

In those days before the trust, I remember clandestine meetings taking place in the Builders (Arms) to discuss what might be done about the way the club was going – very cloak and dagger!

More and more people were joining the Swanmail mailing list and views on the administration of the club were coming in from far and wide; not just in the UK, as the exiled fans who had moved abroad added their views to those who were based much closer to the action at the Vetch. In among all of this, the first discussions of fan ownership started to evolve as people pointed out that generally those who had no connection to a club were in it for personal gain and not for the best interests of a club.

Looking at some of the comments made back then, among them was a reference to Northampton Town. Swansea fans were introduced to a club that, in 1992, had debts of £1.6 million and were on the verge of collapse. They were a club with an unpopular chairman and a club that saw fans dip into their wallets to try and make a difference. A supporters' trust was formed, they forced the club into liquidation through persuasion with one of their creditors, and the funds that they raised gave them a place on the board of the football club. A new ground followed and the lease on that ground has a legal condition that the trust must have a full board representation. This was fan power at its best.

In the Championship-winning season of 1999/2000, it appeared that apathy was perhaps winning the day with Swans fans. Many believed that the administration at the time was no good for the club, but on the field the team were winning week in, week out, and heading towards what would be a division-winning performance.

In among it all, though, were rumours of the club potentially being sold, and through the Internet a supporters' trust working group was set up, initially just a few people who had a vision and a desire to see something different happen at Swansea and always mindful of the success it had seen at Northampton.

In that working group was a dear friend of us here at Swans Trust, Richard Lillicrap. Richard is sadly no longer with us, but it was his vision that brought me to the supporters' trust and it was always informative to read what he had to say. One of my regrets from our recent successes has been that Richard never got to enjoy the good times he so craved when he battled to get the trust idea off the ground.

It was shortly before the last game of that 1999/2000 season that Richard outlined further detail on behalf of the working party and on the back of an announcement that, by the end of May, the club would have a 'dramatic change in its financial structure'. This news set alarm bells ringing and made people wonder why they didn't have more information on their club and how they could go about changing that.

So what was the 'dramatic change' to which Richard referred? Well, in March – shortly before he wrote that article – Ninth Floor had announced their intention to float the Swans on the Alternative Investment Market (AIM).

Richard stated he believed that fans of Swansea could raise far more than the £15,000 achieved at Northampton, but – and he was clear on this point – any monies raised should only be handed over in exchange for shares and full board representation with a cast-iron guarantee that it would continue. He stated that the trust should seek to work with existing owners and any new ones that may appear in the future.

Richard also highlighted the success of the trust at Northampton when he looked back to the 1997 play-off final that saw the Swans beaten by Northampton at Wembley. 35,000 fans turned out from Northampton while Swansea could only manage less than 20,000. Richard believed that much of this was due to the links with the local community built up through the formation of the trust.

It was only a vision, but it was the foundations of the supporters' trust and one that slowly people started to buy into and engage further in their discussions.

On the pitch, things were going well for the Swans, although there was a clear supporter apathy to events both on and off the pitch as the team broke club records on the way to winning a Third Division title, with an average crowd of only around 6,000 turning up at the Vetch to savour the team's success.

That apathy was explained in a copy of *Black Swan* – the fanzine of the time, whose editor, Anthony Thomas, explained,

> What I believe lies behind this apathy is that we appear to have an administration that is so detached from the fans that it feels that the club no longer belongs to us. Possibly the same fans who may have run across the pitch in protest after the mullering by Peterborough a few years back now just shake their heads and stream out as if on prescription tranquilisers. We are now so used to Hamer & Co.'s posturing and tight-fisted policies, backed up by an impressive array of media friends, all 'on message', that we are effectively neutered in the passionate way that we feel about this club.

Black Swan was an extension to a degree of the comments that were being made on the website and the mailing list, and Anthony continued,

> This is why we are prepared to stand up and be counted. We will praise the club to the rusting Vetch rafters if they are doing something right. But we will not shirk from asking those questions that need to be asked.
>
> If you're cheesed off about ticket fiascos, overpricing, poor performances, rubbish food and disgusting Vetch toilets; if you're worried about the lack of ambition and the very future of the club, where else are you going to go to exercise your right as a consumer and have your say?

Now this may not encompass the full ideals of the trust, but it was the view of Anthony, Richard and others like them that was increasing the desire for fans to make a difference and, ultimately, led to the formation of the supporters' trust in Swansea.

But there were more developments to come before things started to change in Swansea. In August, the proposed flotation had not materialised, but Mike Lewis explained to the *Western Mail* that plans were still in place for it to happen:

> Debts of £4.5 million are alarming if you do nothing about them. We have put measures in place to deal with the situation. Nine million new 50p shares are being issued.
>
> The flotation is aimed at making the club more fluid financially, reduce losses, attract shareholders to the new holding company and become viable.

A month later, Steve Hamer was on his way from the Swans, claiming, 'I certainly didn't jump – I was pushed.'

By September, the flotation had still not happened, but a further development unravelled at the football club when Neil McClure replaced Steve Hamer as chairman. 'I would like to thank Steve for his work over the last three years. It is felt with the planned flotation that the chairman of the public company should also be chairman of the football club.'

Hamer, though, was not sounding in full agreement when he had said, 'I certainly didn't jump – I was pushed.'

The flotation of the club was pushed back until October, and Hamer added, 'I always had my concerns about the flotation and the reasons behind it.' He refused to sign the prospectus and his time as chairman was over as performances on the pitch were seeing the team slide towards an immediate return to the basement division.

The planned flotation of the club was quickly becoming the focus of the fans and their fears for the club's future were not helped by reports of legal action by their former chairman, who was demanding up to 7.5 per cent of the flotation. Couple that with the new chairman's view that he would not invest again if he had the chance, but promising that they would deliver the Morfa development and a new stadium, and the need and desire for a strong trust became more pronounced as the fans wanted a further say in the club.

As 2000 turned into 2001, these clamours increased and the foundations of the early meetings were carried forward with the words of Neil McClure ringing in the ears of fans: 'We will make a return on our money. We'll come out of this well ahead but it will take longer.' Fears that the well-being of the club was going to be risked to ensure that a company, controlled by an Arsenal season ticket holder and Norwich City fan, made a return for their investment meant that people were prepared to stand up and make a difference.

And this very much meant that the basic foundations for a supporters' trust were in place. There was, of course, much work to be done, plans to be put in place and a constitution to be written, but the desire and passion was there. It was now just a case of harbouring it into a plan with a clear vision. And little did we know that, as the Swans were relegated back to Division Three at the end of the 2000/01 season, in a little over six months' time, the trust – unformed at that stage – would be at the forefront of a fight to save the club's very existence.

2

The Formation

At the age of six I wanted to be a cook. At seven I wanted to be
Napoleon. And my ambition has been growing steadily ever since.
Salvador Dali, 1904–89

While the foundations of the trust were very much built on the
Internet, and in discussions sometimes via random emails that
the sender never realised would open up a wider discussion about
ownership of the club, the first time a group of supporters actually
sat down together to talk about developing it into an actual
organisation was in the unlikely setting of the Sports & Social
Club at Corus Steel Works in Port Talbot.

It was there that, one afternoon, a very small group of like-minded
Swans fans sat down around a table together with a representative
from Supporters Direct, Dave Boyle, who had been invited to the
meeting to discuss the role of supporters' trusts in football. Dave
had been involved in the trust at Northampton mentioned in the
last chapter and, while it was not appreciated at the time, Dave
would be instrumental in the set-up of the trust in Swansea.

When we now look back, it seems very surreal that the first
official meeting of any trust discussion in Swansea was in a small
back room in the sports club, where Anthony Thomas again takes
up the story:

Many Jacks were at that time blissfully ignorant about the
stripping down of our beloved Swansea City by London
venture capitalists.

This was my idea to finally get people around the table, but I always knew it would be others who would take it on as they had the vision to get the project off the ground. I still wonder what could have been achieved at the trust with input from someone as extrovert with an anarchic ideology and gobby sentiment. The club would indisputably be 100 per cent fan-owned but probably aspiring to finally climb out of the Isthmian League.

My decision to contact Supporters Direct was a result of an article I had read in *When Saturday Comes* that chronicled their work with other clubs of a similar size and supporter base. It was one of those light-bulb moments; and while I did not leap out of the bath, rushing down the street in a trail of enthusiasm and Matey, I felt this was precisely what we needed to form a proficient opposition to the circling raptors.

I contacted Dave Boyle from SD, and invited various luminaries and shakers from inside and outside the gilded halls of cyberspace. This gathering of worried souls arranged in a small room at the Corus Sports Club in Port Talbot. I seem to recall an unusual pre-meeting tension like a summit of old gunfighters waiting for the arrival of Frank Miller's gang, which was apt considering that the club was facing high noon.

Of course, that was my insight. It could have been the fact that the buffet my mother ordered for our meeting had been eaten by the golf section! The meeting was constructive and ran over by a considerable time. I have very little recollection in my autumn years of the discussion points other than this was exactly the direction we should go, and the next steps to achieving it.

From here my input, apart from this meeting was mostly developing an identity for the trust, specifically its mission statement. The Internet became a beacon for the clarion call of opposition, and the mobilisation of hearts and minds was not too dissimilar to the way that social networks saved BBC 6 Music (which, like the Swans, went on to greater things and is now considered indispensable).

Seemingly, the shadowy introverts at the formative meeting were already plotting a course to defeat the evil and save this beautifully flawed football club. I – along with thousands of Jacks – will be forever indebted to them for that.

The meeting ended, and although nothing was agreed during the course of that afternoon, it was the catalyst for the next meeting which was held in the more glamorous surroundings of the Brangwyn Hall in Swansea.

Some of the initial discussions were based around 100 per cent ownership of the club, but this was quickly dismissed as an option with a model of around 20–30 per cent being mooted as the ideal situation for any trust that was to be formed.

It may have not been picked up at the time, but Anthony had also held discussions with his local football club, Port Talbot Town, about a supporters' trust there, but it was not going to happen as the concept just passed them by as they believed that they were already run by fans, so it was something that did not interest them. But it was a different theme when the Swans fans sat together and a two-hour meeting quickly turned into a four-hour session as the enthusiasm to take an ownership in their club spilled over and progression was agreed.

The follow-up meeting to that afternoon in Port Talbot took place on 7 July 2001 in the Brangwyn Hall, where 150 Swansea City supporters attended a meeting that was effectively the first step in those fans aiming to get what so many can only dream of – a stake in their football club.

As well as those 150 fans, the event was also attended again by Dave Boyle, who was asked to address those present. With the benefit of hindsight, the words that Dave used when addressing that meeting were inspiring, but back in the summer of 2001 it seemed a very distant dream as he spoke:

> The fans are moral owners of this great sport.
>   They own the game because they will be there for life.
>   Over the years, football clubs have been badly run because fans have not been involved. Supporters' trusts have been successful to the point that at Lincoln City the club is now owned by the fans.
>   I am not saying that will necessarily happen at Swansea City but this is a step in the right direction.

There were nods of agreement within the audience and people slowly visualised a dream where supporters were part of their football club. Dave's words of clubs being badly run rang true at Swansea, as current owners Ninth Floor were running roughshod over all that was in front of them, and seemingly wanted part of a long-mooted Morfa development rather than the future success of the football team.

The Swans and the First Division seemed a distant memory. Reality said it was less than twenty years since the club had topped the First Division, but ever since we dropped out of the top flight it had been a struggle for the team. 'SWANS – IT'S THE END' was the headline in late 1985 as we were wound up in the high court, but it was back then that the first signs of a fight from the fans surfaced as they played their part in a successful campaign to save our club.

And so we got to the stage where we were back at the Brangwyn Hall and meeting organiser Mike Kent addressed the meeting:

> We are not a predatory body designed to go in and tell the board what to do, we want to own Swansea City itself.
>
> At the end of the day it's not going to happen overnight but we want to get some say.
>
> If this trust is set up now then, who knows, in the future we could help save it from going out of business.

I do not think that Mike knew at the time how prophetic his words were to be, but I do know that he was a massive driver behind the organisation that you see now, and every Swansea fan owes him a debt of gratitude for his work in getting what must have felt an impossible dream off the ground. One of the things that makes me sad when I think back to our rise through the divisions is that neither Mike nor Richard Lillicrap (another major driver behind our trust) were still with us to enjoy our arrival in the Premier League. However, I will state now, and you will see why elsewhere, that without those two we may never have got to where we are, and none of us should ever forget that.

There were fears at the time that the foundation of a trust would rival existing supporters' groups that included FOSCFA, the MAGS (Midlands, Avon & Gloucester fans) and also the London-based Jacks, among others, but Dave Boyle assured the group that a supporters' trust was different.

It was agreed on that day that a working party would go ahead with the business of forming a constitution to set up the trust, and a further meeting was called for two weeks later where a launch meeting would be discussed and the next steps were clear.

The foundations for Swansea City Supporters' Trust had been laid, and probably just in the nick of time, as four days later the news came through that Ninth Floor had sold the club for the princely sum of £1 to then managing director Mike Lewis. It was revealed at that time that the club owed £801,098 and it was a part of the sale that Mike Lewis was to repay this loan to Ninth Floor. A clause was also in place that 20 per cent of any future sale profit was also due to the company.

The club was an unattractive proposition and even the new owner didn't want it for too much longer. He declared, 'I have no interest in retaining my new shareholding, other than to formally allow it to be apportioned to new investors. This has been necessary to conclude ongoing negotiations and I expect to be able to give details of these by the early part of next week.'

With debts so high, it seemed inconceivable that Neil McClure, joint chairman of Ninth Floor, declared, 'During our time in ownership of Swansea City we have doubled the club's turnover, improved facilities at the ground and restored the club to the commercial forefront of the community from a time when nobody wanted to do business with it.' The club had posted losses of £797,000 in its previous half-yearly report!

The need for a supporters' trust was gathering momentum and plans were made for the next meeting that was called for 22 July in Swansea. The meeting opened with news of the further development that Neil McClure had been dismissed as joint chairman of Ninth Floor and there was now no chance that the previous owners would ever take Swansea City back into their ownership.

An open debate was held among those present, who numbered around twenty-five, about what people wanted from a trust should one go ahead and be formed. The obvious goals topped the list with most wanting action and funding to save the club should it be needed and gain a part ownership of the club. It was reported at the time that often exiles would be the most passionate members of a trust, and it was also discussed that should people want to invest in the trust then they would need to have confidence that they were part of the club. It was also widely debated that because of the apathy and mistrust that existed for owners of the club, the fans would have to work hard at this to convince people that the motives behind the trust were good.

Of course, support for the creation of a supporters' trust was not unanimous at the time, and there were those saying that it was not a group of fans that was needed to gain control of the club, but a series of investors, such as businessmen, who had funds to wipe the debts of the club away, as well as to invest in the team. Nevertheless, the foundations for the constitution were done and the meeting was divided into sub-groups of people to consider four key areas for the trust: the constitution itself, the financials, a potential public launch meeting and media relations.

The work was formally underway and the various sub-groups convened their individual discussions, with a further meeting called for 5 August, where the final plans for the launch meeting were to be discussed.

The appetite within the working group was the aim to become at least part-owners of the club, and the vision was clear that this appetite needed to be extended across the fanbase, and that there would only be one chance to get it right, as plans were made for an official launch on 27 August 2001.

Dave Boyle addressed the group with a talk on the benefits of forming the trust as an Industrial and Provident Society (IPS), and the meeting voted unanimously in favour of setting the trust up along these lines, which meant that the working party could set up and sign the constitution.

The sub-group charged with setting the plans for the public launch of the trust set about soliciting backing for it, and they contacted current and past players and managers to get their support including John Toshack, who wrote in August 2001, 'I would like to take this opportunity of wishing the Swansea City Supporters' Trust every success in their efforts to help the club during these difficult times.'

Looking back at these early days, Dave Boyle recalls,

My first memory of working with the Swansea City Supporters' Trust was when I started working at Supporters Direct in late 2000. There was a mailing list that had about fifty people on it from various clubs who were interested in the idea of a supporters' trust.

I recall that there were two people on there from Swansea – one was an American guy, Tony Santore, and the other was Richard Lillicrap. Richard was very keen and posted regularly, but things didn't start happening until around March/April 2001 when the whole Ninth Floor ownership started to unravel. It was pretty clear that they had been sucked in by the football boom that followed Euro '96 where you had things like the Alan Hansen investment fund, which tracked various football clubs.

This caused a huge bubble where people thought that they couldn't lose by investing in football, but of course they did, and that included the owners of Ninth Floor. People like Richard had the view that a trust could make a managed move for the assets of the club if they were willing to sell.

I remember going to the first meeting of the trust at Port Talbot Steelworks organised by Anthony Thomas. It was my first time in Port Talbot and I remember being quite depressed by it all as the clouds hung over the hills. I did my bit at the meeting in terms of what we could offer from Supporters Direct and then left the room and watched the Scottish Cup final as everyone debated whether they wanted to go forward with the idea.

After the meeting finished I was put up for the night at Anthony's house and he took me to the local pub and chippy. I was under strict instructions from my boss at the time to claim for anything as he appreciated that much of our work was done in pubs and fast food outlets. The chippy we visited that night didn't do receipts and I distinctly remember them writing down on a gravy-stained wrapper what we had bought and the cost so I could claim it back.

The next time I came down was the next meeting at the Brangwyn Hall, which was essentially the public meeting to decide if there was to be a trust. This meeting took place because we insisted that it could not just be a group of people who could decide if a trust would be formed and you had to test the waters and see if there was a mandate to form the organisation.

In practice, these meetings were self selecting – those people who thought a supporters' trust was a crazy idea just did not go. But I recall Swansea was the first meeting I went to where a group of people who were passionately opposed to a trust actually turned up to vote against it. That made for an interesting day, not just because of those voting against but also the fact that my zip had broken on the way to Swansea and I was fearful of revealing more than I intended on the day!

Luckily, my modesty was spared, the vote went in favour and we all retired to a pub nearby to have a drink, although the afternoon didn't pass completely without incident as I was taken aback by some comments made to me about my allegiance to Northampton Town and, of course, the play-off final of 1997 was a subject of conversation.

The next time I was in Swansea was at the working party meeting of the trust, which was formed at the previous meeting. I came down on a Sunday and there was the usual kind of energy and enthusiasm in the room with about forty people in attendance, which tended to be the norm at these kind of meetings. There was, though, a bit of a falling out at the meeting about whether the trust should be used as an anti-racist vehicle. There was a feeling at a very early stage that if the trust was to appeal to all supporters it had to put any political allegiances to one side. I could see both sides of the argument, although this did lead to a couple of the early organisers of the trust walking away from the organisation at this stage.

People like Mike Kent were very vociferous on this front, believing that the objective at that time was to form a trust, not an anti-racist group.

With the preparation done and the plans in place for the public launch, it was now all systems go to get the trust up and running with members, and the advertising campaign began.

3

The Launch

Do you know the difference between involvement and commitment? Think of ham and eggs. The chicken is involved. The pig is committed.

Martina Navratilova, 1956–

The opening meetings had laid the foundations for the trust and the launch date was committed to be Monday 27 August 2001 after the Swans' home game that afternoon against Cheltenham.

There was much work to be done, and the various working groups formulated their plans for the launch and set about putting the wheels in motion to deliver what had been for some time just a dream. The question was whether the Swans supporters would now publicly back such a scheme.

However, even as the plans were being discussed, events were unfolding at the Vetch that were to ensure that the momentum and desire for a supporters' trust took on a greater urgency. The club had passed into the hands of Mike Lewis and this was leading to more mistrust (no pun intended) towards owners of the club, which was increasing the calls for the fans to have a say.

Further details were coming out of the club in terms of the dire financial position they had been left in, and there was a realisation that, once again, the Swans were facing a very uncertain future. This increased the efforts of those who were charged with establishing the trust in the public domain.

Among the people who were working behind the scenes to get the trust off the ground there were no major targets, and there was no belief at that point in time that ownership of some or all of the club was high up the agenda. There was simply a plan to get a supporters' trust live in Swansea and create a vehicle that gave the fans a voice, even if it was not going to be able to influence workings at the Vetch.

Tudor Evans was part of the launch working party and he explains,

> The trust as a concept was something I had been aware of since the proposal was put forward by the Tory Party. To be honest, I always felt a supporters' trust should have a controlling interest, as in those early days we felt that all the talent we needed was out there on the terraces and we just needed to utilise it.
>
> I was desperate for change at the club, having been so frustrated with years of neglect and abuse of the fans. I used to rush hundreds of miles from god knows where after working a long day, standing on the North Bank on a miserable wet Tuesday night with a few thousand other daft sods, only to see us stuffed by some poor side. Paying our hard-earned money only to be treated like cattle by a bunch of small town, small-minded, deep-pocketed businessmen who couldn't run the proverbial event in a brewery and were only seeking a few miserable 'look at me' column inches in the *Evening Post*. This all had to change.
>
> For the launch at the Patti Pavilion we had no idea of numbers. We were just thinking about the future and trying to be up and running and ready should we be needed. We looked at trust member numbers at other clubs and calculated that a few hundred members would be an achievement.

Auction items were secured in an aim to raise funds on the evening of the launch and the trust working group secured the services of Kevin Johns to provide the compère services for the evening. The trust was now a constitutionally set-up body, which could accept memberships and donations in anticipation of a day when shares in the club may be available to purchase.

27 August arrived and firstly there was the small matter of the Swans in League action, where around 4,000 turned up to watch the team draw 2-2 with Cheltenham. It was a typical Swans performance of the time – goals from Stuart Roberts and

Matthew Bound seemingly set them on the way to victory, but two goals in the last twenty minutes, the second in stoppage time, denied them the victory that they probably deserved and the spoils were shared.

As the disgruntled trudged away from the Vetch, it was noticeable to watch the numbers that headed West to the Patti Pavilion, where the various volunteers were waiting to greet them and hopefully persuade them to part with their hard-earned money.

For those that had not been involved in the steering group that had brought the concept this far, the amazement was there as to the number of people who were involved behind the scenes, and a report on popular Swans website jackarmy.net noted,

> A well done must go to all that worked behind the scenes to get this going and now it is the responsibility of the fans to help them in taking it forward.
>
> The evening kicked off with John Parkhouse thanking all the people that had helped and donated items to the trust. The microphone was then handed to Trevor Watkins from Supporters Direct who explained the concept of the trust and how it should work.
>
> Messages of support were read out from John Hartson, Max Boyce, Gareth Edwards, Rhodri Morgan AM, Eurig Wyn MP, Steve Hamer, Mel Nurse and Mel Charles among others and the trust was officially launched.

The viewpoint of jackarmy.net continued,

> After a short interval it was time for people to dig deep into their pockets for the auction items, which in total raised around £2,000 for the trust. Top prices on the night were the £600 paid for the signed David Beckham shirt and a signed Swans First Division shirt, which raised over £400.
>
> It was also commendable that two people in the audience donated extra items on the evening. A twelve-year-old lad donated John Hollins boots that he had got at Scunthorpe – these raised over £50 and someone else donated a Martin Thomas Nationwide League top from last season that fetched close on £100.

With a raffle running through the evening and the announcement that a few hundred people had joined the trust on the night, we are sure that the steering group will class this as a massive success and a boost that they can take the trust forward with an AGM now needing to take place within three months.

As people made their way out of the Patti Pavilion, the night had proved that the appetite for the trust definitely existed in Swansea, as those early foundations were finally built upon and the organisation was up, running and ready for a future crisis.

With Mike Lewis continuing his search for a new owner for Swansea City, the momentum of the trust increased and volunteers continued their work to try and get people involved in the concept and add numbers to an ever-growing membership number. Tudor Evans again takes up the story:

It was a hard concept for people to get their heads around – ordinary fans running a club. We all became battle hardened and well rehearsed with the trust concept and patter; we became like Jehovah's Witnesses, all singing from the same hymn sheet, trying to fathom out why others couldn't see it when the concept of the trust was clear, simple and as obvious as the noses on our faces.

Preaching the gospel according to the trust was a soul-destroying, depressing slog each home match. There was also some sniping on the Internet from distrustful, faction-based fans suspicious and accusing. Portraying us as being self-serving publicity-seeking puppets, which as well as being a distraction was really depressing because now as well as committing time and money to go and watch games, we were now having to miss large chunks of the matches giving our time and efforts freely to the trust.

Membership of the trust by 15 September stood at 427, and Tudor and his volunteers were working hard on matchdays to sign new people up from the pubs around the Vetch as well as a table at the entrance to the North Bank. The AGM was set for Wednesday 21 November and income at that time stood at around £7,500 with commitments to donations standing at around £165 per month.

Meanwhile, at the Vetch the Swans were about to change hands again, as exclusively revealed by jackarmy.net on 1 October, when the name of Tony Petty was first revealed to Swans fans. The breaking news read,

> Mr Petty was chairman of Brisbane Strikers but left in April 2000 after a very public battle with the club when he accepted an out-of-court settlement to leave. Mr Petty had at one stage threatened to take the club from Brisbane to the Gold Coast, which brought a big backlash from the fans of the Strikers.
>
> We also believe that he has previously tried to have some involvement in West Ham but this did not go further than trying. He immigrated to Australia in 1999 after previously owning shares in another Premiership club, Charlton Athletic.
>
> It seems as if Mr Petty is a football fan – his reported interest in so many clubs seems to back that up. But he has been described to us as a 'rough diamond', which naturally gives us cause for concern.

It was clear at the time that any new owner of the Swans was going to be treated with a very large amount of suspicion, which only backed up the need for the trust to be strong and work with the best interests of the club at heart.

Twenty-four hours later, it was back to jackarmy.net and a headline that simply said 'Don't Do It Mike', with the confirmation that Petty was about to be revealed the following day as the new owner. The article continued,

> He moved to Brisbane Strikers and this is where we find things that should make Swansea City fans worried. He established himself as chairman and managing director of 'Strikers Football Club Pty Ltd' so that (his words) 'I could get on with running the thing without any hindrance'.
>
> One of his duties as managing director was, he decided, to issue new shares, of which he bought enough to ensure that he had the controlling interest in the club. This action did not go down well and, led by Clem Jones, co-founder of the Strikers, it resulted in court action.
>
> All this eventually led to Petty selling his shares back to the club and walking away with an out-of-court settlement in April 2000.

The article concluded,

> We say no and if we have three choices – Lewis, Petty or Administration, then Administration is the best option we can hope for. What does the future hold now? We cannot answer that, the track record is not good and the one thing that is sure to make the new owners unpopular is the sale of any golden assets – if he starts doing that then he is on a sure fire route to losing friends before he has made them.

The *Evening Post* reported,

> No money has changed hands, but the deal could see Australian football club Brisbane Lions putting cash into Swansea. Mr Petty has also pledged to take over the Swans £800,000 debt to former owners Ninth Floor.
>
> Lions chairman Gary Wilkins and chief executive Lawrence Oudendyk are currently in the city and will report back to their board before making a final decision. The pair head back down under this weekend and hope to confirm their intentions within seven days.

It was clear that the change of ownership was not going to be well received within the fan circles, and discussions within the trust were very much geared towards a stepping up of activities, with strong feelings already circulating over the new owners of the club.

Unbeknown to the trust at that time was that the Swans were less than a week away from being thrown into crisis as the morning of 10 October dawned – a day that significantly shaped the future of not just the trust but the club as well.

Yet again, jackarmy.net takes up the story as they report that Glan Letheran and Ron Walton were sacked from the coaching staff. Nicholas Mazzina, David Romo, Steve Watkin and Michael Keegan were among seven players being sacked while the likes of Roger Freestone, Kristian O'Leary and Nick Cusack were offered significantly reduced terms to stay with the club.

Cusack told the BBC, 'We have been talking to the PFA and to the club to look for ways out of this crisis. The PFA have processes to deal with this sort of situation. It's not unprecedented but obviously the players involved are devastated. But we have to sort something out that is in the best interests of the club.'

The view of jackarmy.net was clear:

Now is the time for all Swansea City supporters to stand up and be counted – don't let the football club get shafted like this. It is our football club and if we are not careful then we will not have one to support if this is allowed to continue.

This was one of the very reasons why the trust had been seen as a good idea by so many and there was immediate reaction with a statement in which trust spokesman Leigh Dineen commented,

We formed the trust to represent Swansea City fans, bring the club closer to the community and secure professional football in Swansea.

The news from the Vetch today is very worrying. Mr Petty has launched a cull on staff and with our present position in the League this is a recipe for Conference football.

I have been inundated with calls today from worried supporters wanting to know what's going on. This is not just from trust members but from a range of Swans supporters – so I think I'm speaking on behalf of them all.

Mr Petty has been with us for less than a week. For all we know he could be gone again in six weeks and we'll be left to pick up the pieces. We'd like him to explain what's going on and what he plans to do to secure the club's future. Until he does, we ask that he stops dismantling the team in what we see as a knee-jerk reaction to cutting the club's budgets. We need answers now and not when we are staring non-League football in the face. If he doesn't want to do that then, as an alternative, we'll be happy to buy the club off him and sort it out for ourselves.

This was the first indication from the trust of our involvement in a battle to save the club and came just a mere six weeks after our official launch. And while that step may have come quicker than anyone involved at that stage would have imagined, it was a step that was important to take and meant that the trust was taking the lead that many would have expected of them.

A letter was composed and despatched to Gordon Taylor, chief executive of the Professional Footballers Association, which read,

Dear Mr Taylor,

The events of yesterday at Swansea City Football Club and the inevitable aftermath that will follow was the reason why the supporters' trust was set up in Swansea on August Bank Holiday Monday, call it a premonition if you like, but we were convinced that the sale of our club to non football people would lead to yesterday's catastrophe.

We now have a membership of almost 600, all dedicated to the future of our football club, our presence is needed now more than ever before. It has been recommended to us by Supporters Direct that we formally contact you to notify you of our existence, and that we should be consulted on all issues relevant to the PFA in matters relating to Swansea City FC. The trust are fully supportive of the players at the club and condemn the sackings and treatment of those players.

We look forward to this matter being resolved to the satisfaction of the players at the club, which in turn would bring tremendous relief to the fans at the club, although I must confess that we would wish to see the back of our 'new owner' (although the Football League appears to have no record of the change of ownership), Tony Petty, an alleged businessman, who is described as an Australia-based Englishman.

The response was fairly swift and simply said, 'Thank you for your letter of 10 October. I can assure you of the full support of the PFA in protecting the future of Swansea City Football Club.'

It was time for Swansea to unite behind its football club and the trust was about to become more focal in that unifying process.

4

The War

We shall not flag or fail. We shall go on to the end.
Winston Churchill, 1874–1965

Events on that Wednesday afternoon in Swansea had seen battle lines drawn and the fledgling trust found itself at the heart of that battle as they became the focal point to which people looked to save the club that was in total crisis, thanks to yet another owner who seemingly was just there for their personal gain.

Swansea was going to unite behind their football club and this was a view shared not just by the fans but by the players as well. Long-serving goalkeeper Roger Freestone explained to the *Daily Mirror* at the time, 'We will have a huge following. We need them to get behind us at this moment. My big concern is that Swansea City survive. But it will because the people of Swansea won't let it die. Mr Petty will not get away with this. I was only with him for a few minutes and now he's gone back to Australia, which is brave of him. Mr Petty has made a grave error and will have to come to his senses.'

The dust had settled after the original blow from Petty and then it was time to schedule the action that was needed. At a time when the trust thought that we could consolidate on our strong start and prepare for our first AGM, it was time for everyone to rally round the club and look to ways in which they could come forward to safeguard the future of the club, which of course was one of the prime aims that the trust had.

A meeting was hastily arranged at Swansea Rugby Club, where the trust, along with local businessmen – all of them supporters

– discussed events at the Vetch. The trust was represented by Nigel Hamer and Richard Lillicrap, while also present on the day were Martin Morgan, David Bradshaw, Mel Nurse, Gareth Keen, Tony Davies and David Morgan. The decision of that meeting was that Tony Petty would be offered £10,000 for the club.

Tony Davies had previously met Petty, and so rang him with the offer, but it was rejected out of hand, and over the next few days the offer was increased to £50,000, which again was rejected by a chairman who was becoming increasingly unpopular.

A further meeting of Swans fans was arranged and it was agreed that a protest rally would be held prior to a game against Brighton, marching from Castle Square to the Vetch Field.

Inside the club, the crisis deepened as one of the star players, Stuart Roberts, was sold to Wycombe, and the PFA stepped in to offer assistance to pay the players – amazingly, an offer that was declined by Tony Petty's sidekick, John Shuttleworth. It was confirmed to the PFA at the time that the Swans would not be able to pay the wages at the end of October, which triggered questions from fans as to how this could be the case, given the home matches played and the transfer fee in – amounting to a six-figure sum – for the sale of Roberts.

The trust went back to the press with a simple statement of 'This is only the beginning', where they informed Mr Petty that the past week's demonstrations were not just a one-off act of defiance and 'he had seen nothing yet.' Membership at this point was rapidly approaching 1,000 and the share fund was growing daily as the clamour to remove him from Swansea City gathered pace.

The trust's Leigh Dineen said,

Whatever Mr Petty has to say over the coming weeks will not disguise the fact that he tried to walk into this club and sack seven players. This act will never be forgotten and fans are unanimous in their condemnation of this.

On behalf of our members and all other fans we ask that the council look carefully at the issue of the Morfa (the site for the Swans' proposed new stadium) and the implications it might have on the length of stay in Swansea of Mr Petty. His motives for coming here are unclear but the Morfa Stadium seems to be at the forefront of his plans. For the good of Swansea City FC, its fans, council taxpayers and Swansea as a whole we implore the council at least to delay any announcements until Mr Petty has relinquished control of our club.

We have grave reservations as to the direction in which our club is heading and we ask that the council support us in our efforts. We do not want our club being labelled with the tag of having the best ground in the Conference.

A further rally was called ahead of the game against Leyton Orient, the second such protest since the 'sacking' of the players, and fans of Swansea were joined by fans of their opponents as well as supporters from Bristol City and Cardiff City, with football united behind a club in crisis, which so often happens.

Feelings were running exceptionally high in Swansea and John Shuttleworth was escorted from a city nightclub after the game against Leyton Orient, and Petty did nothing to improve his reputation with Swans fans as he declared in the *Western Mail* that he had done nothing wrong and he was 'surprised at the reaction that I have got'.

News broke in Swansea that there was the possibility of a quick exit for Petty, with reports suggesting that the lack of a stamped transfer could mean that the board of directors had not approved the transfer to its new owner, and the club may return to Mike Lewis' control.

Lewis himself told the BBC,

If the opportunity was presented to me in such a way that it was impossible for the present owner to continue, under legal restrictions, of course I would take it back. I feel I can make a contribution and if that did occur – it's a big if – then I would call in the people who have shown an interest following Mr Petty's cry for help through the action he has taken. Let's see if the people who have said they would help, and rushed to the defence of the club, are still out there. If they are not, then the football club would quickly go into administration. I understand there are two or three groups of people discussing the possibility of a takeover and those would appear to be the people investigating the legal situation. I have had nothing to do with those groups at all and I have been carrying on as I have been told to do.

Whether a return to a previous bad owner from a current bad owner was construed as hope it did appear that maybe there was a chance – but it was a chance that sadly did not materialise into a hand back from Petty, who was due back in Swansea.

The trust wrote to David Burns, chief executive of the Football League, asking them to 'initiate an investigation into the sale of Swansea City FC and seek a thorough explanation from Mr Petty as to his plans for the club'.

The letter continued,

> We understand from your regulations that, save for issues relating to dual ownership or interest, the League has no involvement in the issue of ownership of member clubs per se, and as such, the League has no formal powers to investigate or enquire. In our view, Mr Petty's involvement at Swansea clearly highlights the flaws in the current situation.
>
> That an individual is able to purchase a football club for £1 without even notifying the League out of courtesy, and is able within days to have brought the club to its knees, is a sorry indictment of the current regulatory powers available to the League. We have heard the argument made that the clubs are freestanding companies that are able to be traded freely, and as such, the League has no interest in the trading of clubs. We are sure that this is not your view.
>
> The good name of football depends on the actions of all its stakeholders. Supporters, players, managers and officials are subject to rules to enforce specific football-related punishments regarding their behaviour when it is considered to have brought the game into disrepute, yet owners are seemingly unencumbered.
>
> We urge you therefore to initiate an immediate investigation in the interests of the supporters, the players and ultimately, yourselves. There have been many examples of unscrupulous owners in recent years and each successive example acts as a stain on the reputation of football as a whole.

The trust were looking at every opportunity to force a change at the club, and were also at the heart of a growing movement of local businessmen who were gathering to try and return the club to local ownership. In addition, supporters were uniting behind the club and further methods, likely underhand, were being applied to increase the pressure on the Swans ownership.

The trust's call to the council had not fallen on deaf ears within the walls of County Hall though, and they refused a request from Petty for financial support for the club. A trust spokesman said,

> Tony Petty has not put forward any rational motives for buying into the club and it is difficult to see how any council, with the whole city to answer to, would be able to support what is happening at the club at present. We expect the sackings of players two weeks ago to be only the beginning. Further decimation of the first-team squad seems certain while Mr Petty remains in control.
>
> The trust would also like to inform its members that our representatives were indeed approached by Mr Petty after yesterday's council public meeting and the focus group are considering this request to meet.

What Petty was looking at during this time was to set up a fans' board. Now, you may argue that it was an ideal position for the trust, as it was part of their aim to have a say within the club, but there was inevitable suspicion with anything that Petty put forward, and it was soon learned that his fans' board idea was nothing more than a PR stunt in an attempt to get fans on side through individuals. Strong characters distanced themselves quickly from the concept and it soon died a death, with Petty becoming increasingly desperate.

The trust were working hand in hand with other people at the heart of the battle to remove Petty, and the next step saw club director Mel Nurse serve a writ on the owner for the Ninth Floor debt of £801,000 that he (Nurse) had purchased from the club's previous owners. The plan was that, upon non-payment by Petty, the administrators would be called in and the club would be saved by the waiting business consortium that had been assembled.

The court hearing came and Mel Nurse was asked to provide evidence that he had the funding to take the club forward should administration be granted. Mel made his feelings clear with a statement that said,

Support the supporters' trust. They will be a big player in the overall picture and the future of our club. To those of you who haven't joined the trust, I appeal to you to join today, to those of you who have, please consider increasing your donations to their share fund.

Get involved, be involved, stay involved. It is your club, you the fans can help to preserve league football in Swansea.

Mel's court battle proved fruitless and Petty won the court case, which kept Swansea City in his control after he paid £100,000 to the court to kill off the administration order demanded by the Nurse camp.

The trust's first AGM took place in the heat of battle in November 2001, where chairman John Parkhouse asked supporters to explore and research all appropriate avenues of inquiry with relevance to bringing them into the public domain in the battle against the current owner, and openly offered the newly formed trust as a vehicle for transferring control of the club to local people, in the promise that the future of the club would be secured.

John continued,

We urge the owner to consider this option either on the basis of a 'gift' to the supporters or the sale at 'nominal value only' to the trust. We stress, however, that we would not countenance anything other than a 100 per cent transfer of the owner's current shareholding and, in relation to either option, would expect the club to publicly announce its proposals via the *South Wales Evening Post*. We, in turn, promise to respond publicly and appropriately. We will not, however, be party to any other form of agreement and will not seek to negotiate with the club.

Outside of the AGM, the trust arranged a further meeting at Clyne Golf Club, where Martin Morgan, George Edwards, Don Keefe, David Williams, Nigel Hamer, Leigh Dineen and Huw Jenkins were present. That was followed up at the Oaktree Park Hotel where Martin Burgess, a director removed from office by Tony Petty, became a member of the working party, as did Gareth Keen.

In early December, Petty issued a detailed statement in which he said,

What we have done has been essential in order to start bringing the club's finances back to a healthier position, and begin the task of attracting new investment to the club.

I'm equally aware that the fans want to have an input into the club. This was recognised too late by the club's previous owners but it is something we recognised from day one.

The supporters' trust in particular have made it clear that they want me to sell them the club. However, I want to go much further. I want to give all the supporters of the club a chance to have ownership in the club. To this end I am going to give away without charge up to a third of the club. For this reason, I am going to give any existing season ticket holder, or anyone who buys a season ticket before 1 January 2002, free shares in Swansea City.

It looked nothing more than a hollow gesture to draw money into the club or – as many believed at the time – his pocket. The need for money was highlighted on Christmas Eve when the club staff were informed that there was no money to pay the wages, and that the PFA had been asked for a loan to cover three months' wages.

Shortly after Christmas, Petty revealed that he was in talks with a consortium of potential buyers with a view to selling Swansea City by the end of January. The trust was clear and swift with its response:

The trust is astounded to find that Mr Petty is attempting to lay the blame for the club's perilous financial position at other parties' doors. The lack of any parties coming forward with investment cannot be blamed directly or indirectly on anyone other than the current owners and their advisers. It is their management, or lack of it, that has seen decisions made that the supporters of this club cannot understand or forgive. The nature and the timing of the players not being paid at Christmas is ample evidence of this.

It is acknowledged that Mr Petty has received offers from local concerns for his ownership of the club. These have generally been rejected out of hand and in many instances, have not even received the courtesy of an acknowledgement – one came from the trust itself. He now claims to be in discussion with a consortium. The trust is aware that this consortium is not the one that supporters would readily link with the club and also, through their daily discussions, have no knowledge of another local group that have an interest.

If this new consortium has no emotional ties with the club, the City of Swansea or even the local area, then we must question what motives they have in wanting to acquire 67 per cent of a football club that is heavily insolvent.

Dave Boyle, though, was under no illusion that what was happening at Swansea was completely different to anything that he had seen happen before:

What really changed everything, though, was Petty's arrival. With Lewis there was only ever the belief that he was an interim measure and there was a belief that he was out of his depth, and I do think he bit off more than he could chew at Swansea, and as the trust were negotiating with him, along popped this Petty character and there was something amazing about what happened next and it was the first time that it happened in this country.

For the first time the Internet was used to change things. While there had been things like Fans United, which had been developing with Brighton's campaign to stop the sale of their ground and things like Wimbledon's attempts to stop Milton Keynes happening, these had been very much pre-Internet campaigns organised through other networks.

What was different with Petty was that he was almost following a manual that generally involved an interview with a local paper promising a new stadium, 25,000 seats and Premiership football within five years. What then would normally follow would be that the local paper would run the 'exclusive' and fans would agree and dream of the delivery of the promise, while being blind to the damage that was normally done in the early days of an asset stripper being in charge due to this initial honeymoon period.

What was happening, though, with Swansea was that thanks to the Internet, Petty never got this honeymoon period. Fans were in touch with people in Brisbane where he had previously been an owner and the Swansea fans were told not to give him an inch. So what happened was from the day he arrived there were people criticising him and saying that he was not going to be good for the club. And of course you had things like invasions of the directors' box and the police telling him that they could not guarantee his safety while he was in Swansea, such was the passion against him and the anger he provoked.

And, as 2001 turned into 2002, it became increasingly likely that the ownership of the club was close to changing hands again. With the trust at the head of many activities and discussions, there was a renewed hope that it would be part of that changeover, despite what Petty's view appeared to be at the time.

5

Victory

You ask, what is our aim? I can answer that in one word: victory at all costs, victory in spite of all terror, victory however long and hard the road may be; for without victory there is no survival.
Winston Churchill, 1874–1965

With a New Year there always dawns a new hope, and that was the case as the trust entered into 2002, with a detailed plan now in place to try and gain control of the club, and a group of local businessmen ready to deliver the club back into local hands.

It was hard to believe that it was just four months since the trust was formed and twelve months previously there had been little more than basic Internet discussion around club matters. So much had happened in the period – the club had changed hands twice, the players had not been paid on more than one occasion, and there had been a crisis of the like that few clubs had ever experienced.

But at the heart of it all there was a new organisation acting not just in the best interests of the club, but in the best interests of the supporters as well. It was a growing organisation with an increasing membership base, almost unanimous support from the fans, and was also inherently linked with the local businessmen who were all in agreement that the trust should be part of any form of local ownership of the club.

Two meetings were called for early January – one at the Patti Pavilion, where supporters were asked again to confirm their vote of no confidence in Tony Petty, while the trust called their meeting on

6 January at Manselton and Cwmbwrla community centre, where members new and old were invited to attend, with the trust looking for increased numbers of volunteers to help man the sub-committees for various aspects of the running of the trust.

There was good news around the corner, as on 8 January a call was received by a member of the newly formed consortium, in which Tony Petty agreed to hand over control of Swansea City to the consortium, and was prepared to give sight of the club finances with a view to completing the deal within a two-week period. While agreement was plausible, Petty was also told in no uncertain terms that it was not to be a lengthy bargaining position with other people. Again, this appeared to be false hope rather than anything concrete, as further rumours suggested that property developer Mel Griffin was the one emerging at the front end of the candidates to take over, which was again treated with suspicion from all quarters of supporters.

Those rumours abruptly ended when Griffin and Petty failed to reach a deal for the property developer to take control of the Swans, and publicly aired their disagreement when they spoke to the press, with Petty claiming no contact for almost a week, while Griffin claimed he had spoken to Petty just four days previously. The fact seemed to be indisputable though: the Swans were still under the control of Petty and there was no immediate end in sight. But how wrong could we be?

Steve Penny, a local solicitor, had offered his services free to the consortium and he, along with Tim Jones, Mel Nurse and David Morgan, travelled to Cardiff on 24 January to meet with Petty. With them they had an offer for £20,000 to buy out Petty from his ownership of the club. The offer was accepted, the deal was struck there and then and the four businessmen returned to Swansea, the club back in the control of local people and the supporters' trust very much a part of this group.

Steve Penny released this statement immediately:

At 10.55 p.m. today, Thursday 24 January 2002, the majority shareholding in Swansea City Football Club Limited and its trading subsidiary Swansea City AFC Limited was acquired from Mr Tony Petty by a local consortium led by ex-Swansea City player and long-time supporter of the club Mr Mel Nurse. Mr Petty and

Mr Shuttleworth have resigned as officers of the companies and have no legal, financial or other interest in the club.

The following morning, the press were invited to the Vetch Field, where Steve Penny, again together with Mel Nurse, David Morgan, Martin Burgess and trust representative Leigh Dineen, met the press, and a more detailed statement was read:

Other members of the consortium are all local people or people with roots or connections with Swansea, all of whom have made a financial contribution towards the acquisition of Mr Petty's shares. The final stages of the consortium's negotiations with the previous owner have taken place under difficult circumstances. For obvious reasons it has not been possible to disclose the identities of the members of the consortium. In particular it could have prejudiced the negotiations with Mr Petty.

Members of the consortium include Mel Nurse, Brian Katzen, Gareth Keen, David Morgan, the Swansea City Supporters' Trust and other donors who presently wish to remain anonymous but who care for the future of Swansea and its football club. Other potential investors are already talking to the consortium and the consortium is keen to hear from others.

The Swansea supporters' trust has taken an active role in the consortium's activities and our deep thanks go to the trust representatives and of course to the loyal Swansea fans who have contributed their time, effort and money to that cause. The trust will continue to have an active role in the future of the club.

The consortium would like to put on record that the city council has been extremely supportive over the past weeks. Most recently, we have been discussing the position of the club's lease at the Vetch, as this is one of the club's lifelines. We look forward to continuing those discussions in a constructive way.

Not all of the news, however, is good. This is only the first day of the club's new life. The financial affairs of the club are still difficult and there is a great deal to be done. This will start with an immediate review of the club's financial affairs. During the recent reign of Mr Petty, liquidation of the club was a very real probability. Until that review is undertaken, it will not be possible to be more specific as to what measures will need to be put in place. In the modern world, the club will have to be run prudently. The supporters, players, staff and people of Swansea can however be assured that everything possible will be done to ensure the future well being of league football in Swansea, which must be good for the city.

A further statement was read on behalf of Mel Nurse:

> I would like to thank all of the people who have helped and who I hope will continue to help us. Nick Cusack, Roger Freestone and all the players, management and staff for their loyalty.
>
> Mel Griffin and his colleagues who made way earlier this week for our bid to go forward. The *Evening Post* and other media for their support including Internet people such as Phil Sumbler and Gary Martin.
>
> The efforts behind the scenes of the PFA and the Football League are much appreciated. There are many others, but I'd like to place on record my particular thanks to the people who really matter at the end of the day, namely the supporters, without whom what now has a chance of happening may never have done so. They can rest assured that Swansea City Football Club will from now on be a club with proper supporter representation and hopefully a new stadium with a loyal and locally based board.
>
> With your help and support this club can go places.

There was also the opportunity for the trust to add their own thanks and an email from Richard Lillicrap to the Supporters Direct mailing list revealed much about how wide the support had been during the battle to win back the club.

> I'd like to take this opportunity to thank a number of people out there without whom this would not be possible.
>
> Dave Boyle, Trevor Watkins and Brian Lomax at Supporters Direct. Without your contribution in getting the trust up and running in its very difficult early days and your subsequent support this would not have been possible.
>
> And endless thank-yous to Leyton Orient fans (Rory and Co. in particular), to Chesterfield Trust, Lincoln Trust, Crystal Palace, Swindon and Carlisle Trust whose paperwork we regularly

pillaged. To QPR, Exeter, Wimbledon and Bristol Rovers, plus many more who provided us with moral and practical support. To Brighton fans, who ran a whip round to provide a symbolic contribution to the players who were told 'no pay' on Christmas Eve. To all the hundreds of supporters across the UK and further who sent messages of support. You will not be forgotten.

We are not everyone's favourite club, but do have a passion for the game and its roots as part of the community. It seems we now have an opportunity to rebuild the club on this basis. Let's hope we have the determination and skills to succeed so we can repay some of the help we have received.

A small victory tonight in a remote corner of the UK. Take inspiration from it. This is also your victory. Let the real work now begin. Richard.

Dave Boyle recalls this moment of victory:

Petty had moved on and the new consortium were in charge with a 20 per cent ownership from the trust. The trust had played an absolute blinder throughout all of this. The trust had been doing interviews left, right and centre and it was a perfect game played by the Swans Trust. And this was underpinned by the shareholders' agreement written by Richard that is a fine piece of fan history. When people talk about what happened at Swansea, this is the document that underscores what happened and is the document that guarantees the trust's role. This was the fundamental vision of the supporters' trust movement – it wasn't enough to just receive plaudits and warm words.

Richard understood the importance of this, and one of the tragedies is that he never lived long enough to see all of this success and plaudits coming through. Every time I see Swansea on TV or good things written about Swansea a little bit of me is sad that Richard is not around to take these plaudits because he, among others, deserved them.

It was for that reason that we were so happy to work with Jenny, Richard's partner, to create the Richard Lillicrap award for services to the supporters' trust movement. Richard was always keen to help others, it was not just about getting Swansea to a good place but he wanted to do it for supporters everywhere.

If anyone ever had an issue or query, Richard was always one
of the first to respond with his words of advice based on the
experiences of Swansea.

He had a lot of respect and friends across the supporters'
trust movement and it was no surprise when he got elected to
the board of Supporters Direct. It was, of course, with great
sadness that I learned of his untimely passing, but I will never
forget the send-off he got from his friends at Swansea when I
went to his funeral.

The trust were handed a huge boost to their finances in early
February when local businessman Gareth Keen handed over his
shares to us. His statement read,

> I am pleased to confirm that I have today given my shareholding
> to Swansea City Supporters' Trust.
>
> The agreement between consortium members guaranteed
> a board seat in return for a minimum investment of £50,000.
> The supporters' trust has been guaranteed a place on the board
> of Swansea City AFC Ltd in the expectation that it achieves the
> £50,000 by 31 March. For the time being, the trust's position is
> secure, however, it is essential that the trust achieve the minimum
> investment level if they are to play an active part in the running
> of the club in the long term.
>
> With my shares, the trust now has a £40,000 interest in the
> club. I urge all Swansea fans to support the trust fully. If you
> are not a member then join, if you are a member then make a
> donation. The trust has to act in the best interest of its members
> at all times. It is a democratic institution and officials are elected
> annually. The only way in which fans can have a long-term stake
> in the future of this football club is via the trust. We came very
> close to losing this club for good ten days ago, so let's all make
> sure that we never find ourselves in that position again.

The consortium agreement to which Gareth referred was signed
by members on 6 February, with trust representatives Nigel
Hamer and Leigh Dineen signing on behalf of the trust. During
that meeting, the other investors not named at the takeover press
conference were revealed to be Martin Morgan, Huw Jenkins,

Robert Davies and the Dineen family, together with Dutch-based Swansea fan John Van Zweden.

The race was on for the trust to raise funds and they announced this in their latest release, which simply said, 'You are going to see a lot more activity from the trust. The next stage is fundraising. The aim of the trust is to get a seat on the board and to do that we need hard cash. Soon you will hear the dreaded thud on the door mat from the postman delivering raffle tickets, which we hope you will all get involved in, be it buying or selling.' The fundraising aspect of the trust was underway in the extra time afforded to them by the consortium to raise the money needed – a deadline that was duly met, resulting in the first trust director on the board of Swansea City.

At the next meeting, the trust board voted on who would take that position, which was on a two-year term, and it was agreed that Leigh Dineen would take the role. He formed part of a management committee that would run the club together with Martin Burgess, Dave Morgan, Mel Nurse and Huw Jenkins, although it was not long before Martin Burgess moved on after it was agreed that he could not offer the club anything that was not already in place, as cost-cutting became a necessity with the club still in a very precarious position.

We were now at a stage that I do not think anyone could have envisaged when the first meeting took place in Port Talbot. Less than six months after an initial launch at the end of August, the trust had a shareholding in the football club and a director on the board. After several years of owners around whom there was much suspicion, the club finally had a board of local people who had the best interests of the club at heart, and integral to it all was our representative, which gave a direct voice to the boardroom for the first time.

The club was nowhere near being on a firm footing, nor were there any guarantees that there was a long-term secure future in place, but we were definitely in a position where the club had a chance, and all eyes turned to the management committee and the trust to see how we would recover the situation and take the club back to the position we all desired for it.

Swansea City had, at last, come home.

6

Control

Some people think that football is a matter of life and death. I don't like that attitude. I can assure them it is much more serious than that.

Bill Shankly, 1914–81

It had been a long few months, which seemed more like years, for the trust as we moved into the hot seats at the club in the early part of 2002 but, as Steve Penny noted in his press conference statement, the hard work was just beginning and there was much to be done.

In his first trust newsletter address of February 2002, Leigh Dineen noted,

> The past three months can hardly be termed 'exciting' but they have proved that when Swansea City fans unite they become a potent force in showing which way they want their club run.
>
> If any good at all has come from the shambolic running of the club in the past, it is the supporters' trust. It goes beyond all expectations that we sit here now, as a body of supporters, with a shareholding in the club, a representative on the board and hence a say in the running of this club of ours. The consortium have, from the start, recognised the major part we can play in the club's future and I would like to thank them, on behalf of us all, for the way in which they have conducted matters to allow us this opportunity.
>
> However, we still need to raise a minimum of £10,000 by the end of March to guarantee board representation for evermore

and it is imperative that we reach this target. On the surface it would seem that the trust has fulfilled its aims, but please can I stress that this is not the case, as we must still all work to 'preserve professional football in Swansea' and also to 'bring the football club closer to its community'. This will need a lot of hard work and funds to do so, but I am sure it will be achieved.

Congratulations everyone – you now own part of your football club!

Trust membership at that time stood at around 1,400 of an average gate of around 3,000 for a club whose future was still very much under threat, given the precarious position it had been left in through years of mismanagement.

And that position was very much unrecognised at the time, prompting trust secretary Nigel Hamer to declare, 'The consortium will need all fans' help in going forward at this stage we don't know the financial mess that the previous owner has left us with, it will not be good, that is for sure. We, the fans, must give them patience and understanding. Let's have big support for the next two home matches, every pound is vital but at least it will be going into the football club bank accounts.'

As the consortium took charge of the football club it was very much a case of learning on the job, as none had direct experience of running a football club, although all were businessmen in their own right. Leigh Dineen had been elected as supporter director and was quick to assume his position within the club boardroom, as well as holding the position of trust chair as voted in by his fellow board members.

Leigh takes up the story:

We were taking on the club completely blind. We knew it was in a bad state because we had been given insights to the club by some people who worked within it, and of course Tony Petty himself said that the club was saddled with massive debts, but we never really knew the full extent of those until we took complete charge at the end of January.

There were no proper filing systems within the club, it was all tables piled high with paper, and it was no real surprise to us when we first saw it to see exactly what state it had been run into.

We had some real dirty work to do when we took over, which was necessary to ensure the club could survive. We needed to get rid of backroom staff. Upstairs, above the club shop, there was the commercial department. Within that department there was a lottery-type scheme being run where, let's just say, the list of winners was always raising a few eyebrows as to the legitimacy of the scheme. That was one of our first moves – to get rid of the lottery scheme.

We stripped the staff at the club back to the bare minimum to survive. There was a girl doing the accounts and just one person left in the commercial department by the time we had completed that exercise, as we looked to cut costs as much as we could.

The club was being run on a hand-to-mouth basis. Things were so bad at times that when I sat down with Huw (Jenkins), when a bill became payable we would look at each other and agree that the only option would be to look to Martin (Morgan), and borrow money from him to cover the bill until money came in from gate receipts or whatever was due. We even used to have Dave (Morgan) getting the float for the turnstiles on his credit card, as we had no money to even provide that on a matchday.

Between myself, Huw Jenkins and David Morgan we divided up most of the workload that was involved in running the club. Realistically, had we bought in the expertise that we needed at this stage the club would not have survived, given the cost that the expertise would have involved. We had more volunteers coming in at senior level as well in Don (Keefe) and Steve (Penny) who were assisting us in keeping the club afloat.

Even as you look back now, when you paid for an item in the club shop at the time it went through Casey's Roofing, so bad was the club's credit rating at the time, meaning that we could not secure the facilities that we needed to be able to accept payment via that method.

Most of the decisions that we took were on a day-to-day basis and it was a little while before we had to make a decision that was something that I would class to be of a bigger issue.

That bigger issue decision came at the beginning of March when the club decided to relieve the manager Colin Addison and his assistant Peter Nicholas of their duties in charge of the club.

There had been reports in the newspapers at the time under the headline of 'Back us or sack us', where it was claimed that Peter Nicholas was looking for reassurances that the club would back their management or risk losing them.

Nicholas was quoted as saying,

We're not going to hang around. If people don't make their minds up, we'll make it for them and walk away.

We're now reaching a situation where certain individuals have got to knock on our door and tell us what is going on. Colin and I have talked and we're not going to let this uncertainty continue for much longer. All of this isn't fair to our families, the Swansea players, the fans or ourselves. I'm not putting a deadline for decision day but we're getting there.

Colin Addison and myself have been through hell since we landed at Swansea last September. Many weaker individuals would have walked away from all the trouble. But despite the difficulties we've battled through. We've been strong together and we have an excellent working partnership.

Interestingly, at the time, the comments were not backed by Addison, who said via an official club statement,

Press speculation over the weekend has not helped the situation. At no time have either myself or Peter Nicholas issued a 'back us or sack us' ultimatum. It's not our style to issue threats, we have been in the game too long for that sort of approach.

We had a long discussion regarding our position with our contracts expiring at the end of August. The meeting was at our request, as we are keen to plan for next season. The new owners have now been in place for five weeks and we feel that the time is right for us to ask the question.

The discussions were very frank and Huw assured us that there is a full committee meeting planned for later this week where the matter will be discussed in full.

Leigh adds,

It was a Tuesday night and we were heading to Shrewsbury for a game, and we were split between two cars having a conversation on the mobiles via the hands-free kits in the cars. It was during that conversation that we took the decision to sack the management team just before the team lost 3-0 that night.

It was Huw who informed them of that decision – he was always the communicator when it came to the football-related decisions, whereas I tended to communicate anything that directly impacted on the commercial side of the business.

No decisions were taken solely though by any of us, and this was one of those where we were in total agreement, especially as the club was facing the CVA around the corner.

The decision was not well received by Nicholas, who claimed that the club had gone back on an offer earlier that week of a new contract:

On Monday we were called in to be offered a two-year contract, but it had changed by Thursday afternoon.

Basically they put it down to financial matters. They said the footballing side of it was fine but it was purely financial. Colin and myself had contracts until the end of the season and I was very disappointed in the decision.

I feel very let down by the management committee and especially their leader, Mel Nurse. He is supposed to be a football person but it didn't appear so on Thursday.

Colin Addison added, 'Peter and myself wanted to finish the season, despite what we were told. We wanted to be on the team bus that went to Carlisle. Jenkins stopped us and told me to go immediately. That man has been in the game five weeks but I've been in football almost fifty years – he's not going to dictate to me.'

Mel Nurse was quoted at the time as saying about the committee decision, 'In the last week we have received a letter from the Inland Revenue for £300,000 which wasn't a bill but a demand. These are the sort of things we are dealing with from day to day and why we have had to take these actions and get rid of Colin and Peter.'

Leigh had briefed the trust board ahead of the decision being made public, and via a trust statement he added,

The group has wrestled with this issue long and hard. The club is still in a perilous financial condition thanks to the chaos caused by Lewis and Petty. And there is more than one winding-up order on the club and little likelihood of any further windfall income to tide things over.

Their contracts amount to well over six figures a year with substantial expenses. There is simply no way that the figures add up. The club just can't afford to pay at that level for its management team.

The club followed up their decision by placing Nick Cusack and Roger Freestone in joint charge for the weekend game against Carlisle, as the management committee moved on to face their next battle, which would dictate whether the club had a long-term future.

Ever since the consortium had gained control of the club they had been determined to bring under control the club's finances, amounting to debts into seven figures, thanks to the mess left by the previous owners. The set-up of the club was structured such that the consortium money was invested in a new holding company – Swansea City 2002 Ltd, which in turn owned the 99.15 per cent shareholding that had previously belonged to Silver Shield.

Leigh explains why this was a necessity:

The money was held by the consortium rather than by the club. Had it gone into the club then it would have been used to pay the debts. There was the football club and also a company set up by Silver Shield when they wanted to float the club on the AIM.

The money that was put in was to make sure that we had enough to go to CVA (Company Voluntary Agreement, i.e. to pay the debts at the reduced amount). We also planned to sell the lease back to the council after completion of the CVA, which would give us enough money to see us through to the end of the season, which in turn would satisfy the Football League. We had no choice but to go to CVA or the club would not have existed.

Just twenty-four hours after the removal of the management team came the confirmation that the club would be seeking a CVA with creditors two weeks later. This brought about some criticism from fans as to the timing of the discussions, but with the sale of the

Vetch lease also announced, it was explained in a trust statement, which said,

> The way in which this week's news has been broadcast leaves a lot to be desired and Leigh has delivered that message back to the consortium in strong terms. But it is clear now that the announcements regarding the agreement with the council over the sale of the Vetch lease, the dismissal of Addison and Nicholas, and the disclosure of the CVA were subject to critical timing and, without all three pieces of information, a full understanding by fans was not possible. The council has insisted on total confidentiality, but the cash deal on the lease was fundamentally important to the whole plan. If the CVA had been announced before the agreement with the council then the lease would have become void and valueless.

The total debts of the club were revealed at the time to be over £1.6 million, with the single biggest creditor being Mel Nurse at £701,097, and the Inland Revenue accounting for another £249,271 of the debt. Also on the list were John Hollins, Colin Addison and Martin Burgess, as well as Mike Lewis.

Leigh once again takes up the story:

> The CVA took place at the Marriott Hotel where Dave Morgan, Gary Stones and myself were at the front of the room presenting the proposal on behalf of the football club. The simplistic offer was that we would pay five pence in the pound to everyone bar the Inland Revenue. We needed 75 per cent agreement to the proposal, although the reality was there was no proposal to agree as the alternative was administration for the club and all creditors getting nothing.

The outcome of the CVA discussion was that 92.4 per cent of the creditors agreed and the immediate short-term future of the club was assured as they entered a CVA for a two-year period – the amount of time it was agreed it would take to repay the Inland Revenue. The good news on this front also was that those that voted against the CVA were bound by the majority decision, and there could be no winding-up orders issued by them.

A trust statement was again promptly issued and Leigh declared,

This is truly a moment to be celebrated by all supporters. For the first time for many, many years we know exactly where the club stands and there are no outsiders with the power to tell us what we can and cannot do with our club. From now on it is up to us.

There are many challenges to be faced and a lot of hard work to be done. That starts tomorrow. But today we celebrate. The slate is effectively wiped clean and the consortium in partnership with us, the supporters via the trust, can at long last start the process of rebuilding our club.

I would like to acknowledge the support that has been given by so many local businesses and by other individuals. I believe they understand that this action was essential to enable the club to go forward.

With the immediate future of the club secure, the management committee moved forward with the day-to-day management of the club, and approached Brian Flynn to be director of football, to which he initially agreed, but then backed out when the club refused to agree to his other terms. Those terms were detailed via a club statement:

At the last minute and without prior warning, Brian demanded that the club also appoint Kevin Reeves in a role that, as Brian well knew, was already earmarked for Nick Cusack, as new player-coach. The club owes an enormous debt to Nick, who has provided outstanding leadership through the period of major upheaval under Tony Petty's reign. The club is not prepared to cut Nick loose. Loyalty to him is of paramount importance and the club will not be held to ransom and sacrifice his future. Brian knew this from day one and the club is extremely disappointed that he has approached matters in the way he has. It is for these reasons that the club has terminated talks with Brian Flynn. The club will, quite simply, not be held to ransom by any manager before he is in position and especially not over the future of such a devoted and loyal player and future manager as Nick Cusack.

That loyalty was reaffirmed shortly afterwards when Nick Cusack was offered the permanent post as manager, although little did anyone know just how much that loyalty would be tested in the months to come.

It had been a chaotic time for all involved in the club, and the trust involvement was immense, as in a four-month period they helped secure the club's future and, for the first time, were involved in the day-to-day decisions that affected the football club. This was the vision that was first explored around twelve months earlier, a vision that nobody at the time would have believed would come to reality quite so quickly. But it had and Swansea City was partly owned by the supporters. As it should be.

1. Mike Lewis (*left*) and Tony Petty (*right*) outside of the Vetch.

2. John Shuttleworth (*left*) and Tony Petty (*right*) – a rare moment of smiling at the Vetch.

SOCCER: Trust vows to battle on for survival of club it loves

We'll keep fighting

BATTLE PLANS: The newly elected board of trustees gather at the AGM of the Swansea City Supporters Trust at the Patti Pavilion last week.

THE Trust wishes to publicly reassure its members, the supporters of Swansea City Football Club and all persons genuinely concerned for the future of the club, that it will continue in and indeed increase, its endeavours to help return the club to local ownership.

The Trust board remains of the view that the current club owner does not retain the public and commercial confidence of the people of Swansea and that despite recent public statements made on behalf of the club it is doubtful that the pledged investment will materialise.

These factors, the board believes, make the current ownership untenable within the city.

It is already reported that other financial problems exist within the club and we believe that these will not be addressed through pledged investment nor by the owner who has readily admitted to not having funds himself.

This leaves the club with one alternative and that is to systematically sell key assets and players and staff to fund its commitments. The inevitable consequence of

SWANSEA City Supporters Trust held its annual general meeting last week amid all the court wranglings surrounding Mel Nurse and Tony Petty. Since the meeting Nurse's petition to put the club into administration has failed but the Trust is unwaivering in its quest to ensure the survival of the club. Here it sets out its aims for the future of Swansea City as it sees it.

such actions will result in a weakening of the squad, an inability to compete at current league level and ultimately will put the club at risk of relegation from the league and/or liquidation.

We believe that all persons concerned with the club, be that privately as shareholders commercially, should now seek directly from the owner, whatever

written assurances they believe necessary for the secure continuance of their involvement.

The demise of the club, to whatever degree, will reflect negatively on all concerned including the City of Swansea.

We also call upon the elected body of the City and County of Swansea to declare publicly the level of its concern and to confirm what actions it intends taking.

During this continued period of uncertainty, the Trust will endeavour, for information purposes, to explore and research all appropriate avenues of inquiry with relevance to the club and, wherever possible, to bring any concerns or information to the public arena.

To the current owner, we would say that local public opinion and commercial confidence is already against him and that this situation will not improve as local resolve on the issue is increased and the lack of proper investment is proven.

The opportunity is now here to transfer control of the club to local people at no further cost to the parties concerned.

We openly offer the Supporters Trust as a vehicle for such a transfer, with the confidence that the future of Swansea City Football Club will be secured.

We urge the owner to consider this option, either on the basis of a 'gift' to the supporters or sale at 'normal value only' (given the original purchase cost) to the Trust. We stress however that we would

not countenance anything other than a 100 per cent transfer of the owner's current shareholding and in relation to either option, would expect the club to publicly announce its proposals via the *South Wales Evening Post*.

We, in turn, promise to respond publicly and appropriately. We will not however be party to any other form of agreement and will not seek to negotiate with the club.

The Trust and its members and all other supporters of Swansea City FC have the club's survival and its place in the future of this city at heart.

The opportunity now exists for the owner to place the club in the hands of those that care and with the knowledge that he will have played a part in that future.

This action could go some way to improving the unfavourable impression made so far and would guarantee that he will have made a significant contribution to history by ensuring that the club becomes one of the few in the Football League to be returned to the fans and the local community.

When the dust settles, he may be remembered more for his final generous gesture, rather than his earlier unpopular actions.

We earnestly hope that he grasps this.

> To the current owner, we would say that local public opinion and commercial confidence is already against him and that this situation will not improve as local resolve on the issue is increased and the lack of proper investment is proven.

3. The *Evening Post* – a week after the first trust AGM, November 2001.

4. The fans march through Swansea in October 2001.

5. Nigel Hamer (*left*) presents club director David Morgan (*right*) with our first investment.

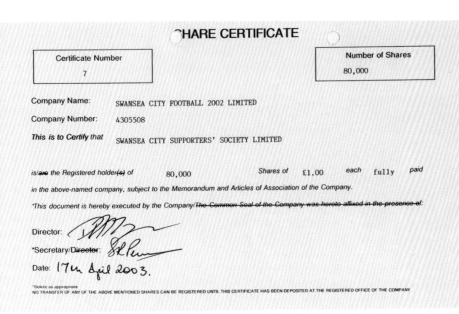

6. Our first share certificate issued by the holding company.

7. The now famous 'Battle for Britton' logo.

8. The Swans squad at the bowling night, 2006.

9. Standing Room Only at the Carmarthen fans' forum.

10. The Ivor Allchurch statue outside the Liberty Stadium.

11. The queue outside the Liberty at the first open day, 2006.

12. Helpers at the open day, 2006.

13. Brendan Rodgers at his first fans' forum, 2010.

14. Gerhard Tremmel and Michael Laudrup at the bowling night, 2012.

15. Nathan Dyer, Player of the Year 2011.

16. Swans legend Keith Walker screws his plate into the Wall of Fame.

17. Stars of the past at the Wall of Fame unveiling.

18. The forums head to Port Talbot.

7

Fundraising

Give us your f*****g money.
Bob Geldof, 1954–

After the trials and tribulations of the 2001/02 season, the club embarked on the following campaign full of optimism that the corner had been turned. The club under its new owners had spent the summer, with new manager Nick Cusack, strengthening his squad with the addition of some experienced faces. Cusack had released eight players soon after the completion of the previous campaign, and over the course of the summer had signed nine new faces for the club, as he rebuilt a squad that he believed could challenge at the top end of the division.

It did not take long, though, for thoughts of a comfortable season to subside as the first grumblings appeared around early September that the manager was not the man for the job, and the rumours resurfaced that he was about to be replaced with Brian Flynn, despite the club statement from the previous season that stated their loyalty was to Cusack and they would not see him cast adrift from the football club.

The Swans headed to Boston in mid-September as the rumours of the managerial changes gathered pace, and they seemed almost certain to be confirmed as Brian Flynn and Kevin Reeves turned up at the game to watch the Swans slip to a 1-0 defeat, a result that left them anchored at the bottom of the Football League.

The following day, the news that everyone expected was confirmed with a club statement that said, 'As a result of discussions between the board of Swansea City and player-manager Nick Cusack, the club announces that steps have been taken to make new appointments to the club's management team. Everyone has recognised that strengthening of the management team is necessary. We are delighted to announce that Brian Flynn has been appointed as Director of Football with immediate effect.'

It was a complete U-turn for the club given the statement issued the previous season, when they stopped talks with Flynn, but it was a sign that the club's management, which included the trust, were not prepared to gamble the club's future, and would make a decision that may be viewed as unpopular within some sections of the fan base.

A trust statement read,

> In order to avoid any doubt, the trust board wishes to make its members and fans aware that it has been kept fully informed at all times by Leigh Dineen, its supporter director, as to the nature of any discussions that have taken place.
>
> While any announcement concerning changes of personnel will be made as appropriate by the club, the trust board, as always, is committed to keeping its members advised of developments and will do so via the usual channels.

It was clear from a read of the Internet forums that the decision was not met with universal approval, and the trust statement makes it clear that there was real criticism of the organisation for the first time since we were formed a little over twelve months previously. However, this was an open regime and Leigh himself was quick to respond to the criticism. He confirmed that the trust board was aware of the state of the football club and reiterated via the forums why the decision had been taken to remove Cusack from his managerial duties.

Through it all, the trust were badgering their supporter director to arrange a meeting to view plans for the New Stadium (as it had now become known). They were invited to attend a presentation from the council where the plans for the stadium were revealed, and it was announced that work on the stadium would begin in October. The trust board raised many issues that had been passed on to them by fans, including disabled areas and standing areas, and the council agreed that they would keep the trust board informed on all things regarding stadium progress. However, that appeared to be a false promise and less than two months later the trust were active in the *Evening Post* letters page as they questioned delays to the start of work and called for a public show of no confidence in the officials of the authority.

There was also good news for the trust, as they were awarded second place at the annual supporters' trust conference for the best trust – behind that of AFC Wimbledon – and it was Richard Lillicrap who was 'delighted to accept this on behalf of all those who have worked tirelessly and often without thanks to get us where we are today'.

It was around this time as well that the first signs of concerted fundraising from the trust came about, although this time it wasn't a call for money that was required but a call for members to collect tokens from the local newspaper. Huw Cooze wrote at the time,

> It has been brought to my attention that the *Evening Post* are running a competition for a £25,000 minibus. All we have to do is collect tokens that appear in each edition of the *Evening Post*. The trust as a body are 1,500 strong and should be in with a fair chance of winning, especially if everyone pulls together.
>
> If won, it could be used for both youth and first team for training purposes, along with other projects organised by the trust for the children in the community.

It was the first sign of things that were to come, as Leigh Dineen explains:

> The trust was being seen as a fundraising arm for the club. Whenever the club was looking to raise funds for whatever reason at the time, they would tend to turn to us and see what ideas we could come up with.
>
> We have several examples of successful campaigns that were trust-led, which include the now famous 'Battle for Britton' campaign, which in turn was a follow-up campaign to our original one, 'Let's Stop Moaning and Get a Loan In'.

And that loan campaign was launched in October 2002 as it became more obvious that the club was going to be involved in a season-long fight against relegation from the Football League. New players were needed and the trust wanted to play their part, as their appeal stated:

> Money is being asked for but the question must be asked as to how much is League football worth to you? A lot, we hope, and that is why we must do all we can to help the manager and the players.
>
> The aim is to raise a minimum of £375 per week for a three-month period. This might mean three loan players for a month each or payment for the first three months of a loan player that remains until the end of the season. We are asking that people set up a standing order for a minimum of £5 per week for the three-month period.
>
> Now is the time to dig deep – two months down the line may be too late. This scheme will allow us to see the outcome of our efforts on the pitch, and we will obtain shares in return for our hard work and generosity.

Leigh adds now,

> Some of these campaigns may not have been met with universal approval from other shareholders, some of whom remained a little suspicious of the trust at the time, and felt that we were being given an unfair advantage of being able to get more shares through the generosity of the fans. In hindsight, maybe that view was right, but it was necessary at the time as the club were still strapped for monies, and this was one of the reasons that the trust was there.
>
> There was a suspicion in many quarters of the motives of the trust and what our overall aims were, and within the club it took a few years to shake off that suspicion as the two bodies worked closely together with the same aim in mind – the safeguarding of the future of the club.

The trust campaign received a welcome boost shortly afterwards when Roger Freestone, the club's long-standing goalkeeper, chipped in with £375 towards the campaign. Roger explained,

> I have been at this club for over eleven years and they have provided me with so many happy memories. I have turned down

chances to leave because of what the club means, not just to me but also to the supporters.

It would break my heart if we were to slip out of the Football League and I commend those with the vision to set up a scheme like this. If this scheme can make the difference so that the manager can strengthen the squad as he thinks fit, then it will be money well spent, and I urge others to dig deep and give what they can afford and together we will do everything we can to keep Swansea in the Football League.

As the campaign gathered momentum, Brian Flynn was quick to act and it was a now familiar name that was first to arrive as Alan Tate signed on loan from Manchester United, with Flynn lauding the player as 'a footballing centre-half, a good passer and someone who distributes the ball well'.

In an interview with jackarmy.net, the trust's Nigel Hamer confirmed the success of the loan scheme:

The scheme was launched in October and has raised £28,000. There have been 230 individual contributions, not all from trust members or Swans fans, and six businesses have made the maximum contribution. The trust adopted Alan Tate as the player whose wages we were initially going to cover until the end of the season, but such has been the success of the scheme that we were also able to contribute towards a second players wages, and that was Marc Richards.

The scheme remains open, although the initial impetus has fallen away. We are currently working on a reinvention of the scheme.

Leigh was also looking at changes within the club and he adds,

As a club we started to experiment with admission prices as we wanted the fans to become the twelfth man. We slashed admission prices for the visit of Lincoln in January. Crowds had been between three and four thousand for most of the season but we wanted fans to back the club more, and over five thousand attended the Lincoln game, and only once more that season did we drop below that figure and that was only by around a hundred.

It wasn't the only campaign that we ran that season. There was a ladies' day and we did kids for free for the Wrexham game as well. We were all well aware as fans what a difference a busy Vetch could make, and we were ready to do whatever we could to preserve league status within the city.

And League status was secured after a nervous final-day victory over Hull City, sealed – maybe somewhat ironically – by a hat-trick from James Thomas, one of the nine people that had been brought into the club the previous summer by Nick Cusack. The club had fought a successful fight once again and taken the decisions needed to make that fight a successful one. A change in manager may not have been the most well received at the time, but through their belief and a little help (well, £28,000 worth of help) from the trust the fight was a good one and the Swans were still in the League.

Due to the success of that scheme, and as alluded to in the interview before the successful fight against relegation, the trust launched what has now become known as one of its flagship fundraising schemes – Battle for Britton. This is one of the schemes that is still referred to now, but a trust communication at the time read:

Roman Abramovich went to the wrong SEA. Had he come to SwanSEA instead of ChelSEA then there might be no need for this article – or indeed the appeal that it fronts. The fact that he chose Chelsea doesn't lessen our ambition at Swansea though, and that is where you, the trust member, and you, the fan, come in.

The trust board believe that Brian Flynn has put together a pretty useful squad that can push for automatic promotion. We also know that come Christmas or just afterwards, he is going to have to delve into the transfer market, whether to cover injury, loss of form or plain old suspensions. This is a fact.

Other clubs with rich benefactors can do so at the drop of a hat. We, on the other hand, with the consortium of local businessmen, cannot, so it is up to us, yet again, we believe, to give the budget a boost at the appropriate time.

As we know, the League this season has brought in wage capping for Third Division clubs. As one of the better-supported clubs, this should not affect us as badly as it will some clubs, but come May 2004 we don't want to find ourselves in a position of 'almost but not quite'. We need funds to be available so that Brian Flynn can play an ace or two when the situation arises.

Last season we very successfully ran the 'Let's Stop Moaning and Get a Loan In' campaign and in truth, its success exceeded our wildest expectations. This money was ploughed into the club, paid towards Alan Tate and Marc Richards' wages and gained the trust, on behalf of all supporters, a greater share in the club.

Apart from the very obvious contribution made by these players in helping the club avoid relegation to the Conference, the not-so-obvious side issue was that the money donated effectively freed other club funds and enabled the management to bring in a number of other key players and the rest, as they say, is history.

One of those key players was Leon Britton and it is true to say that he captured the hearts of Swans fans with his tenacious energy-filled displays. So much so that the close-season 'demand' was that the club make every effort to sign him permanently. When this became a distinct possibility, the trust board decided to help the course of events and out of that decision emerged the 'Battle for Britton' scheme.

It was our initial idea to run the scheme with the intention of paying Leon's salary for the first year. In return, the trust would receive one share in the club for every pound paid over. This of course further increases the trust's shareholding in the club, giving it, on behalf of all supporters, a greater say in how things should be done at the club.

The call at the time was for fans to pledge £5 per month for a year, although smaller and larger donations were of course welcomed. The scheme was backed by the player himself who added,

I'm more than pleased to help the trust with this campaign and am flattered that they and the fans consider me to be a role model for it.

It's clearly an important issue for the club, as the more money available to the manager, the better the prospects of him strengthening the team when it really matters.

There is an air of optimism in the dressing room already and the players are determined to do their best to get this club to the top. The supporters' trust evidently plays an important part in the club, not only raising funds but also uniting supporters, so this scheme is well worth supporting, The supporters at this club are phenomenal and I sincerely hope they sign up for this scheme in droves.

This scheme is definitely the iconic one of all those we have run over the course of twelve years since formation. In the build up to both the play-off final and the Capital One Cup final, it was the one latched onto by the press, given the fact that Leon is still here.

'Maybe,' adds Leigh with a smile on his face, 'we should still be paying Leon's wages now, seeing as it is just about our fault that he is here in the first place!'

Current supporter director Huw Cooze takes up the tale:

As a trust board we thought back at the time that, having seen the initial success of bringing in Alan Tate and Leon Britton, there was a future in loan players were the club to prosper, so we came up with the 'Let's Stop Moaning and Get a Loan In' scheme, which was to raise £28,000.

If you think about it, then, that would pay two loan players for the best part of six months when the average wage we were paying at the time was around £500 per week. If you compare that to now it would be unlikely to cover one player for a fortnight, but to a club in our position it was strengthening the squad quite significantly.

The second scheme was as much of a success as the first one, as fans dug deep to take their club to the next level. I firmly believe that there are few clubs that could succeed with a scheme like this, and it just seemed a natural step up, having won the battle to first take back control and secondly to stay in the Football League. Things were on the up.

8

Change

Change is inevitable. In a progressive country change is constant.
Benjamin Disraeli, 1804–81

Changes within the trust have become few and far between in
recent years, with the stability that has grown throughout the
club both on and off the pitch. The early months of the trust saw
substantial change as early architects of the trust concept elected
not to be part of the organisation going forward, so we took our
place on the club board with Leigh Dineen representing us as part
of the management committee.

In June 2003, Leigh's position became that of vice chairman
as the club moved to make appointments at board level, with
Huw Jenkins taking on the role as chairman and declaring to the
official site,

> We felt that now was the right time to appoint a chairman and vice
> chairman because it will help the club move forward and grow.
>
> With the foundations now in place, it will give the club the
> right image, plus leadership, to take us in the right direction,
> and I believe that, in partnership with the supporters' trust, we
> will go from strength to strength. Decisions have, and will be
> taken in the interest of the whole club, not just one or two,
> and we will not gamble on the future of the club we love for
> anything. When we took over, the Swans were sinking. Now,
> with the club holding its own, it is time to move forward and
> continue making progress.

For some time, the fans and our members had been calling for the club to make appointments to take on the key roles within the club, and interestingly at this time there were also rumours that the trust might get a second director on the board as a result of the changes, although this was to be in a non-executive capacity. An associate director was appointed from within the trust ranks, initially Paul Morris in 2003, who was succeeded in 2004 by Huw Cooze.

Our position within the club retained this profile until it was announced in April 2006 that Leigh was to stand down at the start of the next trust year, although he retained his position on the board due to his own shareholding. Then trust chairman Ron Knuszka commented,

> It is with great regret that Leigh informed me of his decision. Having worked tirelessly with the trust over the past five years, Leigh now feels that it is time to step backward and concentrate on his role within the football club together with his family life.
>
> As a trust we will always be indebted to Leigh for his dedication to both the trust and the club, and we most certainly would not be where we are now if it were not for that work. Naturally, we will remain in close contact with Leigh as the trust looks to work closely with the club, and I offer our heartfelt thanks for his commitment of the last five years.

That wasn't the only change of that summer, as Ron had also decided to stand down as chair of the trust, meaning we had to make another change within the make-up of the board. It was at that point that I was fortunate enough to be elected by the board members into the position of chairman, and my first task in that role was to oversee the voting process to elect our next supporter director. When you look back to the appointment of Leigh as director back in 2002 it was a pretty straightforward decision, and he had been the natural choice to take that role, but by the time he stood down in 2006 we had some strong faces on the board who were well equipped to take on the role.

After a close vote, the decision of the trust board was to promote Huw Cooze from his position as associate director into the role of supporter director. And at the time, I think my words summed up that we felt we had made the right decision:

The supporters' trust would firstly like to thank Leigh Dineen for his hard work in the past five years in his role. We are confident in appointing Huw that we have made the right decision, and while Leigh is a very hard act to follow I am sure that our members will find Huw equally as approachable and determined to see the club growing.

It was always going to be a challenge for Huw taking on this role, as he was joining a board that had worked together for almost five years, and had overseen the promotion of the club back into the third tier as well as the move to the Liberty Stadium. Naturally, through his work on the trust board since its inception, he already knew the personalities on the board, but there is a big difference as I am sure you can appreciate between knowing someone and working closely with them on a day-to-day basis.

I'll let Huw take up the tale at this point:

My role as supporter director on the club board started in September 2006 after a two-year stint as the trust's associate director.

Joining the club board was rather daunting, but I already knew some of the characters, having made myself familiar with them through invite to the boardroom for the odd game, as part of the trust agreement from the outset of the consortium formation. I had shadowed Leigh Dineen for a number of years and was ready and proud to take on the role. At my first board meeting I had to wait outside while they formally invited me in, a bit of protocol but nothing I could not handle.

I was unsure what to expect, but to my surprise and delight the topics discussed were similar to what was being discussed on the terracing and in bars across the city, it was a pleasure being asked an opinion on something that was very close to my heart and surprisingly easier than I thought. Being voted in to take over from Leigh was a massive honour for me, a rough and tumble Morriston boy, but I was proud to do it then and I still am now some seven years later. I felt that I had done my apprenticeship with the trust and the club and was ready for the challenge.

I'm sure that there are people hoping that I am about to lift the lid on some boardroom struggles and disputes but that really isn't my style. I think, though, it is fair to say that the board do not agree on everything, but that should be no surprise. How could it be possible for nine people to continually have the same opinion on everything? Like any board, we debate many topics which involve the club and in the main it is the club that is the winner when we reach a decision that we run with.

One thing that has been levelled at me and the trust over the years is that the position of a supporter director is nothing more than a token gesture. It is worth remembering here that we have a position on the board because we have a shareholding that warrants it. It could be possible at other clubs that appointments are a token gesture, but that is certainly not the case at Swansea. I would say that on average I speak to Huw Jenkins at least four or five times a week and of course more when there are bigger decisions or events going on. Huw and I also travel to away matches together on a regular basis and usually end up having a beer or two on our return. Huw himself will tell you that as board members we are not just colleagues but we are also a group of friends, and I think that is an important factor in our recent successes.

The good news about the club board is that we are all supporters of this wonderful club of ours and we all think broadly along the same wavelength. I know that up to our move to the Liberty Stadium, I had never sat down in a stadium (Coventry in 1982 being the only exception), and I know that all the fellow board members have done their time standing on the North Bank and terraces up and down the country.

I have worked closely with Huw Cooze over the years, having held this position for the same length of time, and I have to say that he has grown into his position within the club, and I question whether we could find anyone better suited to the role. I know that it hurts him when people make the comment that his appointment is a token gesture, and I see at first hand a lot of the work that he does within the club, which brings me nicely on to the question of what he does within the club and what decisions/initiatives he has been involved in. Many of the tasks that Huw works hard behind the scenes on are not necessarily ideas that have come from the trust board, but most definitely ideas that he has taken to the club and delivered to our fan base as benefits to them.

I felt it was important here to give you some insights into the role of the supporter director, so again it's over to Huw:

I am now involved in more and more meetings, especially since reaching the Premier League. There was a time prior to this that perhaps one meeting a week was the norm but it is more than that now. Recently, I was asked by Huw Jenkins to take up a new role that has been stowed upon us by the Premier League – that of Supporters Liaison Officer. This role comes into play under the UEFA Club Licensing and Financial Fair Play Regulations and all clubs had to appoint one of these to ensure better communication between club and fans. In reality, this position is just an extension of what I have always done and involves me in not just looking after supporters' needs, but looking into subjects such as racism, bullying, disability and supporter experience. Earlier this year, I visited the Amex Stadium at Brighton and, while we get a lot of things right at our club, we can always improve. Brighton are a great example of a club who get a lot more right and I'm looking forward to learning more from other SLOs when I attend a two-day conference later this year at the Cardiff City Stadium.

It can be quite frustrating for us at times as we don't own our own stadium. I recall that we managed to get Huw Jenkins over to the Riverside Lounge for the first fans' forum to be held at the new stadium. Some of the questions he was asked that evening he would have been able to answer in relation to the Vetch, but they were now out of his hands with Stadco running the stadium, and that, I think, took us all some time to get used to. Going back to the stadium itself, we had numerous meetings with the council when it was in the planning process and it was a devastating blow when we heard that the capacity was being cut from 25,000 to 20,000. I attended an open meeting with Berwyn Price, who was project manager of the stadium build, and we let him know in no uncertain terms that the decision lacked ambition and was foolhardy, but we were shouted down when his reply was 'be grateful for what you are getting', which I think was typical of some of the (lack of) foresight that went into the stadium itself.

However, the stadium is what it is and because of the fact that we have a third party running the stadium it is about making sure that everyone is singing from the same hymn sheet. I attend regular meetings with the stadium manager, the customer service manager, and head of operations, looking at ways to improve the supporter experience. I also meet with the caterers, FMC, and guys from the ticket office to make sure we constantly evolve and that we never get complacent.

So what kind of things can these meetings lead to? Well, we had regular meetings a few years ago on consistent problems with the stadium. It was at our insistence that the anti-slip paint was put onto the stadium floor, and we also convinced the council to reconfigure the toilets in the East Stand to try and ease some of the congestion experienced at half-time. We also sorted the issue of the pinch point near the foot bridge over the River Tawe, and the controversial 'turn right' policy after the game in the East Stand was something we campaigned tirelessly on over a long period.

On top of this, I meet regularly with Ugo Vallario from the Travel Club. I have known Ugo for over forty years and he does a fantastic job in arranging the travel for away fans, but we all have to work together and meeting with Ugo ensures that the ticket office and customer service people are also in regular dialogue.

We have recently set up the Disabled Supporters Association, which is spearheaded by Ian James. I have attended many of the initial meetings to help get this off the ground and I know that Ian has some good people helping him here and we have ensured that the club give him their full support.

Other meetings include 'Show Racism the Red Card'. This does exactly what it says on the tin, and while we are lucky at Swansea in that we don't have a problem with racism it is always good to stay on top and abreast of the latest developments on this front.

The recent survey to support the club's extension planning application was organised by me, and with the help of fellow trust board members and the Travel Club we delivered a massive report that has strengthened the planning application, which will hopefully get more seats in the Liberty. I also represent the club at SAG (Safety Advisory Group) meetings. There is plenty going on at these meetings and there are often twenty around the table, with a representation from the Premier League, police, ambulance and fire services as well as stadium management and council officials. You may recall an evening fixture a few years back where many were ejected from the stadium for standing, and it was through SAG that we gained the relaxations that we currently have towards standing in the stadium. There was a belief in the early days of the stadium that maybe some of the enjoyment was being taken away from being a supporter, but it is key here to remember that everyone was adapting and learning about a new environment. I believe that work around meetings such as after that game has got us to the stage where we appreciate what the stadium regulations say, but we have found the happy medium that we all desire.

One of the benefits that I believe our promotion to the Premier League should gain for us at the club is a future generation of Swans fans. If you look back to the John Toshack era it gave us a generation of Swans fans, many of whom are still coming through the gates at the Liberty. We need to get the same benefits from this rise to the top flight and there are several initiatives that I work with currently to increase the likelihood of this happening.

Leigh Dineen and I are heading up a new initiative to involve more children in our club as well as sport in general. Tony Pennock, head of youth development, and Linden Jones, head of the community trust, will be working together to make sure every child in our catchment area is involved in Swansea City in some capacity. We hope through this to be able to deliver a clear message and perhaps spot the potential next star. This has already been part of what we do at Swansea City but now we hope to intensify this programme and you will see more on this in the future.

In terms of building our fanbase beyond Swansea, we have made inroads in Holland thanks to John Van Zweden, Denmark and South Korea thanks to Michael Laudrup and Ki Sung-Yueng, and we are also growing all over Asia and America as well as South Africa. We have good ties with an American Youth Team – North Shore United – and in Cape Town, where Brian Katzen recently presented a seminar on Swansea City to business leaders from that part of the world. And of course thanks to our Spanish contingent we are gaining fans almost daily there as well.

I also sit on a steering group along with fellow director Steve Penny, looking at ways on how to improve Swansea as a destination through our involvement in the Premier League. This is a tourism type body that doesn't really have much to do with us as a club, but if the city can have a spin off for what we are doing at the football club then who am I to argue.

I am sure you can see, from the initiatives that Huw is involved in, that he is extremely busy in what he does for the football club and this does not include the extra activities we ask him to champion within the club as and when they arise. However, these meetings are just part of his role and I'd guess very much hidden from the public domain until the output from them comes into play. Alongside this, there are examples over the years of events that have taken place at the Liberty, which have had Huw very much in the foreground as one of the driving forces from the club's side.

One of the examples of this would be the family days that have taken place at the Liberty Stadium. The first of these was against Carlisle late in 2006. The family day was actually the third initiative in a bigger campaign for the club entitled 'Fans of the Future' and followed up on 'Free Season Tickets for the Under-8s' and a 'Kids Go Free' scheme that had been running. The concept behind this family day was that kids could watch the game from the South Stand for just £1. Huw worked strenuously on this event, galvanising us as a trust board to support him at the match itself handing out sweets, balloons, freebies to the families attending the game and also organising face painters, clowns and the club mascots to enhance the day. It is interesting to note at that time that the club had 1,173 season ticket holders aged sixteen or under and, as with most of these events, attendance was good at this particular fixture.

These events were always hard work, but well supported by trust volunteers as we packed the back of the South Stand giving out sweets, freebies and helping out with the face painting and other activities that took place on the days. Huw was instrumental in working on three or four of these events when we were in League One in particular, which were always well attended, much like the opening one against Carlisle.

After the seven years that Huw has worked with the club board, I would go as far as to say that the trust now has a far stronger working relationship with the club board than we have ever had. We have mentioned before about people seeing the appointment as something of a token gesture, but having been chair of the trust for that period I have seen that very much not being the case, and I can assure all members that we take forward their issues and they are heard and there are many examples – as Huw has mentioned – where that voice has made a difference in terms of what we do.

As with many things in life, the trust have come through changes, particularly around this appointment, but we came through it stronger, and I hope that this particular chapter has given you a good insight into the work that we do within the club via our director.

9

Community

Fans are the heart of football.

John Charles, 1931–2004

As a supporters' trust, we have four main aims that we set at the very outset of the organisation. These are as follows:

1. To maintain a professional Football League club in Swansea.
2. To have an elected supporters' representative on the board of Swansea City Football Club.
3. To raise sufficient funds to buy a stake in the club, in pursuance of the aims above.
4. To bring the football club closer to its local community.

I do not think there are too many people that could dispute the success that we have achieved in aims 1–3 since our formation, as you have seen elsewhere in this book.

But one of the reasons why Swansea City is the success story it is is thanks to our delivery of point 4: to bring the football club closer to its local community. I suppose that, to an extent, in Swansea we have always been lucky in that the football club has always been relatively close. Swansea, in reality, is a very small city, and if you speak to players from previous generations then they will tell you that they have always felt as if the club was close to the fans.

But at the trust we wanted to take that closeness to the next level, and that provided us with us some challenges as to how we went about it. You will already have read in this book about our formative months and how the fans completely backed the club in the fight against Tony Petty. It was, therefore, on the back of the consortium gaining control of the club that we wanted to build on the closeness that had developed between the fan base and the club during that battle.

One of the first concepts that we used to bring the club closer to its community was that of a fans' forum. Interestingly, this had been tried a couple of times by the Silver Shield regime and largely organised through the unofficial websites. These were probably one of the first opportunities that fans of the club had to question those that were running the club, but all too often at these events questions were vetted beforehand and answers were given just to questions that were submitted for inclusion on the evening. I had attended a couple of these, under the control of Neil McClure at the club, and I always believed that they were nothing more than lip service to say they had been done, rather than offering anything that would give people a viewpoint into how the football club was being run.

But with the new consortium in charge, this was always going to be different. We had local businessmen in charge of the club and, for the first time, we had a 20 per cent stake owned by the supporters through us at the trust. Therefore the fans' forum was introduced, and in April 2002, Leigh Dineen announced that the first one of the new regime would take place, with places limited to the first 100 people. The trust reserved forty of these for their board members and fans affiliated to supporters' groups, with the other sixty places drawn by lot from the people who applied to be part of the forum.

Leigh said,

The management committee have said all along that the club will be run in a much more open manner than in the past and this is the first step to achieving this. I think there will be some experimentation before we get the format right. If the meeting is too large, some important people will get 'lost' in the audience; too small, and people will feel excluded.

We are very grateful to Kevin Johns who has, once again, agreed to compère the evening. There will be no vetting of questions so it should be a lively and entertaining event. We have

asked Kevin to keep everything moving along so as many topics
as possible can be covered on the night.

Because of the limited numbers available, we also opened up our
website for people to submit questions in advance, recognising
that many would be unable to attend and also due to the large
number of exiled fans at the club. Leigh added, 'I'm delighted
that we have the opportunity to answer the many questions that
I'm sure the supporters will have. This type of communication
between the management committee, the supporters' trust and
the fans is the only way forward if we are to achieve our aim of a
community orientated club.'

At that first forum, fans in attendance met with Nick Cusack, who
was in charge of first-team affairs at the time, and representatives
from the management committee in Steve Penny, Leigh Dineen,
Huw Jenkins and David Morgan. Those in attendance answered
questions as openly and honestly as they had promised from a
whole range of subjects put to them by the fans.

Picking out some of the highlights of these questions, one was
the revelation that the transfer embargo that had been put in place
because of the CVA only had seven days left to run, although, as
was pointed out, any potential new signings that were about to
arrive would be subject to strict budgets put in place as part of
the CVA.

There had been press reports at the time of a bid for the club
from Bo Ekland, which generated the response that the consortium
would step aside if it was in the best interest of the club, but there
was a comfort factor when David Morgan advised that there were
'safeguards in place to make sure the club does not fall into the
hands of anyone who doesn't have the club's best interests at heart'.

The management committee also advised that they had seen all
the plans and proposals for the development of the Morfa Stadium
and that a confidentiality agreement was in place to not reveal
more details of the plan, but they had been assured that the club
would move into their new home by May 2003 (a timescale that,
of course, never materialised and was put back by two years).

There was good news when it was confirmed that the club
would be returning to their traditional black-and-white strip that
summer, ditching the red and white introduced by Silver Shield,

while the committee were critical of the FAW decision to take the final against Cardiff to Ninian Park, thus denying the club of vital income at a time when it was most needed.

The biggest question of the night, though, was as to whether there would be any civil or criminal proceedings against Tony Petty or Mike Lewis for their management of the club, to which the answer was that no decision would be taken until the auditors had finished with their assessment of the club accounts.

From our perspective, this was a huge success and provided the foundation for many fans' forums to follow. As Leigh had said prior to the event, we were learning all the time, but the feedback from those present was essentially positive and allowed us to consider future events going forward.

However, there became a dilemma with fans' forums going forward in getting people to attend in sufficient numbers. The vice president's room at the Vetch was the venue of choice but people did not turn up to support the forums as much as we would have liked, and we started to question whether we could continue these events moving forward. As we have learned though over the years, a non-attendance is not really an excuse for not organising and it is important from our perspective to continue to provide these events. We have also learnt over the years that the guests we have at these events are all important, and that outside factors do not always help us. I remember us heading to Stebonheath Park in Llanelli for a fans' forum a few years back, where there were less than ten people in attendance despite the presence of club captain Garry Monk and Alan Tate, but torrential rain on the night just discouraged people attending and I think we counted more trust board members there than 'guests'. But to contrast that event we have had hugely successful forums in Port Talbot, Gorseinon and Carmarthen, as well as the recent ones that we have organised in London, which have been massively popular among our exiled fans in the South East.

It was in the days of Ron Knuszka as chairman that we started to take the forums on the road, and although we initially started with different venues in Swansea, we slowly extended these out to the further reaches of where our support came from to try and encompass them. I mentioned earlier one at Carmarthen, which I believe was our most successful 'road trip' of all, but that was purely down to the guest that we had in attendance. It was somewhat aptly timed for the forum in that it took place in November 2005, at a time when a certain Lee Trundle was lighting up League One with some incredible displays that had seen him less than a week before score a wonderful goal against Yeovil on a night when the Liberty Stadium witnessed its first streaker. Trunds was flanked that night by Ron as our chairman and also by Leigh, who was still supporter director at the time, but for once there were very few questions for anyone outside of the star attraction, with over 100 people crammed into a relatively small room at Carmarthen Town AFC, which simply did not have enough seats to cater for us all.

A couple of months before that night at Carmarthen we held our first fans' forum at the Liberty Stadium, just a month or so after the club had officially moved in. Early teething problems that the fans experienced with the stadium were always going to be high on the agenda, and it was Huw Jenkins and Kenny Jackett who faced the supporters' questions on that occasion. Huw, as we have grown accustomed to at our forums, was as honest as ever with his answers and he admitted that he shared many of the frustrations of the fans, but openly admitted that they could not be changed overnight and that there were difficulties in dealing with local government.

These early-season forums are the ones that we have stuck with over the years, and forums have become a once- or twice-a-season event in the main. Traditionally, we now host a forum in August/ September at the Liberty, where we invite the manager, chairman and a few of the new signings to face the fans' questions, and they have grown to be hugely popular with over 100 people there on the evening. As the club have progressed through the divisions, I have found this to be a bigger plus point from our perspective, as not many clubs at this level offer this kind of interaction with key people within the club, and it should be something that supporters encompass, which in the main they do.

The other additions to our calendar of fans' forums are recent ones that have been held in London. Traditionally these are organised on the eve of a Swans weekend match in London and again we tend to have the chairman invited to these events. Unlike the ones in Swansea, we double them up as a fundraising event with tickets sold for attendance, but we are yet to not have a sell-out at one of these events, despite the cost, and they are definitely something I can see us continuing in the future. One thing I learned from my own time as an exile was that if you can get close to your club then you will take the opportunity when it arises. The events in London have been well supported and show that the Swans fan base is strong and passionate, no matter where they may be based.

Our move to the Liberty Stadium in the summer of 2005 gave us some new challenges, particularly around the fact that so many people felt close to the Vetch Field, but the first season at the Liberty – as we stated earlier in this chapter – gave us plenty of teething issues that were a new thing to us as supporters. In the summer of 2006, we aimed to take on two projects that would bring the club closer to the community. The first was an open day at the Vetch that we wanted to arrange to coincide with the twenty-fifth anniversary of the club's promotion to the First Division. Unfortunately, we were unable to proceed with this because the city council – who had been so supportive of the idea – after full legal consideration, felt that the risk of injury given the state of the Vetch at the time was too great to allow the event to take place. From our side, we were disappointed to hear this, as we wanted to give everyone one more chance to say goodbye, but it just wasn't to be. As a result we turned our attentions to the open day that we were arranging at the Liberty Stadium, to give supporters their first look inside the stadium.

To open the doors of the Liberty to the supporters took some planning but, after many months and meetings, we eventually agreed that we would open the gates on Sunday 20 August. I have to admit that we were unsure whether people would turn up or not, but we pressed ahead with the arrangements and had opportunities for people to take their photographs with players in the dugouts and dressing rooms, as well as with the Johnstone's Paint Trophy and FAW Premier Cup that we had won the previous season. We arranged face painters, clowns and trade exhibition stands, as well as a mini-forum where a couple of hundred people turned up twice to listen to Kenny Jackett give a talk on his hopes for the new season. I remember on the day walking out to open the gates of the south-west corner of the stadium to let people in, and seeing several hundred queuing and knowing that this was always going to be one of our most successful events. What we didn't expect at that time was the total attendance on the day, which exceeded 5,000 people, leading us to repeat the open day in 2007 with my comments at the time being, 'It was tremendous to see so many of our supporters attending last year's event and we hope that people will support this one in as many numbers. Roberto has been extremely busy over the summer and this is the first chance for many supporters to meet his new recruits and of course listen to the thoughts of the manager as the new season gets underway.'

And while the second open day was a success, it never reached the dizzying heights of the first one, and it is not an event that we have repeated since. I do wonder whether the time is now right to repeat it, especially given some of the improvements that have been made to the stadium in the six years that have passed since the last open day, so perhaps it's time to watch this space – you never know!

While forums and open days have been hugely successful for us, we have also held a wide range of social events and none more so than our bowling night, which has become one of the most eagerly anticipated social events on our calendar each year. It was back in October 2003 that we launched the first one at what was then the Megabowl in Parc Tawe. The idea was a simple one: we hired out the venue and sold lanes for people to attend on the night. Each lane would have a player/club representative with them and the idea was simply to give people a good night out while they had the chance to meet the players of that time. The first event was a complete sell-out of all 208 places available at the time, and this has now become an annual event.

As time has progressed, we have made small tweaks to the format of the evening, but we know that when it comes around then it will sell out quickly as it's a relaxed evening that, much like the forums, would not get repeated at too many Premier League clubs. Interestingly, there is much competition between the players as to who wins the player's award for the highest score, although few of them want to win the skittle that represents the lowest player score on the night!

The winning bowling team are also the proud recipients of the Richard Lillicrap trophy, which sits proudly on display at the Liberty Stadium all year round, and from our point of view simply adds to the enjoyment of the event. It has seen slightly reduced numbers now (it tends to be around 160) but will sell out within hours of going on sale, which tells you how popular it is.

In 2007, we added another social event to our annual calendar, when, following an idea by trust board member Ian Roberts, we hosted the Swans' first annual Awards Dinner at the Liberty Stadium. The event took place on 21 April 2007 and was attended by around 300 people. Leon Britton was the big winner for us on the night, scooping all three main awards (fans player of the year, players' player of the year and away player of the year), but it was the introduction of an award that we initiated that probably gives me the greatest pleasure each year. I believe that our club is unique in terms of the way it is set up and the way that we have always had a substantial number of people who work within the club, often on a voluntary basis. These people, I believe, encompass many of the ideals that we stand for as a trust, and therefore it was with these people in mind that we set up the supporters' trust Lifetime Achievement award, which is designed to recognise those people who give their time and commitment to the club, but often without any form of reward. I don't think I will ever forget the look on Major Reg Pike's face that night as we announced his name as the inaugural winner of the award and he proudly clutched his trophy all that evening. Reg was a matchday host at the Swans and looked after the mascots extremely well, and was most definitely a deserved winner of the award, as have been the other recipients to date – Professor David Farmer, Mel Nurse, Ugo Vallario, Gwilym Joseph, Kevin Johns and Huw Jenkins.

We were assisted in the organisation of that awards dinner by Steve McLelland, who worked with us on the trust board, but after he stood down and returned to his duties with the executive fundraising committee the event became a joint event with them, and is another that sells out within hours of tickets going on sale, which, when you consider we had over 600 people there last year, is no mean feat. At the time of writing this book, we are in the process of setting up a 'roll of honour' board in the Riverside Bar at the Liberty, which will proudly show all the people who have won our lifetime achievement award as well as the coveted fans player of the year award.

These are the main events that we have organised in our pursuit of bringing the football club closer to the community, but they are not exclusive events by any means. We have organised quiz nights and race nights on top of these, as well as events that are listed in other parts of this book that were arranged for specific fundraising events.

One of our most ambitious projects, I believe, was the launch of the West Wales Transport Scheme back in 2005. The scheme went live in February and was designed to make life easier for fans coming from Pembrokeshire, Ceredigion and Carmarthenshire. The aim was to give these supporters affordable travel, and with costs starting at just £4 it would be the cheapest way for fans in this area to travel initially to the Vetch and then, the following season, the Liberty Stadium. Pick-ups started in Milford Haven and worked their way through to Carmarthen as the last stop and dropped off in Swansea at 1 p.m. Evening games were also catered for, with the last bus returning from Swansea around 10 p.m. for these games. The concept was a simple one, and one that proved popular for the period that it ran. At times, there was almost a full bus coming from West Wales for the game and John Young, our trust board member at the time, was delighted with the progress that it was making. Unfortunately, though, as we became more used to travel to the Liberty Stadium, the administration work behind the scheme became a logistical nightmare and the demand was subsiding. The club helped us by financially supporting the scheme, but eventually we had to call a halt to the bus scheme, which was a disappointment, but necessary at the time.

Most recently, we have also discussed as a group the potential opportunities that we have to support local junior league football. We believe that there is a fantastic opportunity for us to link our organisation with the many junior teams that play football on a regular basis throughout Swansea and our surrounding areas. Our thoughts work around a viewpoint that not only will this raise our profile within the community, but it will also potentially make a host of junior footballers feel closer to our football club, which can only ever be a good thing. When I look back at my time of starting to support the Swans, it was at a period when the football club was on the rise and a lifetime's passion was born. That can be the same for today's juniors, and therefore we want to do our bit to try and harness that through this potential partnership.

I do believe firmly that as a trust we have worked hard on our community links and the various items that we have discussed in this chapter highlight that. You would argue at the moment that it is easier for the club to be part of the community, especially when you consider what their rise to the Premier League has been estimated to be worth in the local economy. However, we retain a principal belief from our set-up that there is still work to be done and I do not suspect there are too many Premier League clubs who interact with their fan base as much as we do. It is something that we will continue to work on and part of our work that we are extremely proud of, and I would also say one of the most enjoyable aspects of our work as a trust board.

10

History

Nobody is forgotten when it is convenient to remember him.
Benjamin Disraeli, 1804–81

For many of us who grew up watching the Swans and, in particular, those who sit on the trust board past and present, our time following the Swans started at the Vetch Field. For those of you fortunate enough to visit the Vetch, it was never the most attractive of football grounds and it was most definitely a ground that had past its sell-by date by some distance. But for us it was home and steeped in the history and tradition of Swansea City.

It was the ground that witnessed some memorable occasions and games and once held over 32,000 people for a game against Arsenal in the 1960s. The rust was all through the ground and there were parts of the ground condemned, never to be used again, but that did not take away any of the character of the ground and was something that was possibly lost forever when we moved to the Liberty Stadium back in 2005.

A new, modern stadium is part of football in the twenty-first century and I would certainly argue that had it not been for the stadium move then none of our success in the eight years since we moved would have happened. But the move in the summer of 2005 took away many of the characteristics that captured our history at the old ground.

The Harry Griffiths bar that sat behind the centre stand was no more; the Mel Nurse bar that was behind the North Bank had also gone with it, meaning that the new stadium was 'clean'. I use that word because that was a phrase that was used when we first moved to the stadium as essential to attract naming rights. The name of White Rock Stadium had been in play while it was being constructed, but this was dropped during the period leading up to the move as the council searched for a naming sponsor and stated that the title should be 'clean' at that point, so we were gifted the New Stadium, Swansea, for a short period until October 2005 when Liberty Properties secured the naming rights.

As a trust, we were worried that the move to the stadium would take away some of our history and with the stadium being heralded as potential use for seminars, trade shows and pop concerts, we wanted to be in a position where Swansea's history, which was closing in on 100 years, was celebrated at the stadium for visitors new and old to see.

It was with that in mind that, in late 2004, an idea was hatched to celebrate part of that past at the new stadium. The chairman at the time, Ron Knuszka, had this to say:

> During the half-time interval at one game, a few of us 'oldies' on the North Bank started talking about some of the Swans' great players of the past. Not too surprisingly, Ivor Allchurch came out on top and it was unanimously agreed that Ivor was one of the best – if not the best – players ever to wear a Swans shirt.
>
> It was suggested that it would be a great tribute from Swans fans to commission a bronze bust of Ivor and have it placed prominently in the new stadium, not only as a mark of respect for the great man but also to provide an important historical link between the old ground and the new. The cost to commission a sculptor to undertake this project is in the region of £5,000.
>
> Following enquiries with the club it has been agreed that if a bronze bust were commissioned then it would take pride of place in the New Stadium.

We had the go-ahead from the club, so the next move was to seek the permission of Mrs Esme Allchurch and family to bring to fruition the half-time chat about the memorial to Ivor. After a family discussion, the Allchurch family gave their approval for a bronze bust. At this time, trust secretary Nigel Hamer joined Ron Knuszka in finding a company who specialised in this line of work.

We were directed to a firm of designers, sculptors and casters in Farnborough, Hampshire. Over the next few months, we met with the designer, Peter Bellchambers, at Esme's home looking at hundreds of photographs of Ivor's playing days to allow us to get a front view, side view and back view of Ivor's head profile so that the artist could produce a maquette.

The fundraising was underway, and if there was one thing that we had learned in the early years of the trust, it is that Swans fans were always prepared to put their hands in their pocket when it came to celebrating the past, present or future of their club, so events were organised. Early events saw over £200 raised at the annual ten pin bowling night with a raffle and, more impressively, over £2,000 was raised at a race night held in early 2005, which put us halfway towards our target very early on in the campaign.

It was not long before the desire to produce a bronze bust of Ivor had extended to become a statue that upped the target for fundraising to not far short of £20,000, a figure that we knew was extremely challenging but definitely achievable.

Internet website scfc.co.uk also jumped in with us to arrange a memorial golf day at Langland Bay Golf Club, one of the city's premier golf clubs, which set an objective to raise a further £2,000 for the event. Again, Swans fans turned up in their droves to support the event, with over twenty teams of four playing and over 100 people sat in the clubhouse in the evening listening to the speeches from Ron as trust chair and also John Allchurch, Ivor's son. Auction items came from far and wide and included a signed shirt from Alan Shearer of Newcastle, one of Ivor's previous clubs. Along with Alan's shirt came a letter which read, 'There is no need to remind fans here at St James' Park of the tremendous impact made by the late Ivor Allchurch when playing for United. I am pleased to offer you this signed shirt of mine in the hope that it will increase your funds for his memorial statue outside of your new home. Alan Shearer, Club Captain.' The figure of £2,000 was eclipsed as over £3,000 was raised for the statue fund and we were gathering momentum.

It wasn't just Swans fans that were contributing to the statue – a letter of support came in from Sir Trevor Brooking, while the Football Association of Wales generously donated £5,000 and further donations came from Swansea City Football Club and the City and County of Swansea Council to boost the fund.

Several bucket collections also took place at matches and raised over £1,000 and Ron Knuszka remembers one collection vividly:

> The bucket was being passed along the line and a small boy asked his grandfather who the picture was of the man on the collection bucket. 'That's Ivor Allchurch, a true gentleman and the best player ever to have played for the Swans,' came the reply. The boy had clearly never heard of him but his hand went into his pocket and he took out the few pennies that he had and put them into a bucket. Things like that bring a lump to your throat and confirm that you are doing the right thing.
>
> We also did several bucket collections at the entrance to Swansea Market and I remember an elderly woman who had walked by, stopped, returned and put a pound coin in the bucket. She then explained that she had contributed in memory of her husband who was a keen Swans fan and a great admirer of Ivor.

Amazingly, the fund grew and grew until such time that we had raised over £21,000. In October 2005, prior to a home game against Oldham Athletic, we were able to unveil the statue outside the ticket office. Several hundred Swans fans, among official dignitaries and Ivor's family, were all present at the unveiling and Ivor stood – as he stands today – proudly outside the stadium looking out towards the Vetch site that he graced with such skill. Again we look back to Ron's comments at the time:

> It has been a long, hard year in collecting for the statue and we would like to thank everyone who has given their time and money to the cause. However, it is only fair that we mention that the original sculpture for the Ivor Allchurch statue was by Michael Field, whose speciality is sporting portrait work which is possessed worldwide by collectors in twenty-three countries.

The one thing that I think disappointed us was the size of the statue, which is a life-size statue of Ivor, but it was only after the event that we were informed that it should probably have been 1.5 sized to give a stronger impact. But having said that, the statue of

Ivor is now an iconic symbol at the Liberty Stadium and regularly features on football shows and their features of the club. The plinth for the statue was kindly donated by Swans season ticket holder Michael Isaac of George J. Isaac & Sons.

One of the other things that the move from the Vetch Field gave us was a thought as to how we would commemorate the old stadium that we were about to depart. When somewhere has been your home for over ninety years, you don't just want to leave with a whimper, and there should be things that you want to retain as memories forever way beyond the point when the stadium is no longer standing.

The project was not exclusively trust organised – there was assistance from many people such as Tudor Evans, Peter Stead and Huw Bowen, among others – but it was very much trust-led as Stuart McDonald, our current treasurer, explains,

Casual conversations involving interested fans had taken place and certain individuals were gradually directed towards one another. A tentative – probably alcohol-induced – conversation on a coach trip on the way home from Rochdale in May 2003 was followed by a couple of exploratory chats over the next few months and the idea was conceived.

The original thoughts of all of us never wavered – it was determination to produce a quality commemoration of the ninety-three years of Vetch life. Conception to birth was to be a long path, but we were on our way. We first 'formally' met in August 2003 with the original group of people augmented at various stages by others, who were either able to bring different skills to the table, or were simply available to lighten the increasingly heavy workload.

An early meeting with the Swans board saw us gain their approval, without which we would never have started. Initial meetings spent much time debating the vexed question of a name for the project. A whole host of quirky and gimmicky titles were considered, and considered again until, eventually, we came back to the aptness and simplicity of THE VETCH 1912–2005. We had seen what other clubs (Manchester City, Hull, Sunderland, Darlington and Stoke, to name a few) had done but we wanted to do something different, something unique, that would capture what the Vetch has meant to generations of Swans fans and the people of South West Wales, and was a celebration of the life of the Vetch, not specifically of the Swans, on which there had already been several excellent works.

The idea of packaging all the mementoes within a special box, which would itself be very much an intrinsic part of the project, was enthusiastically agreed upon by all. We had obtained a copy of the Manchester City 'box', which inspired us by its quality but we set our stall out to surpass that achievement. Whereas theirs was a voluminous photographic book in quality packaging, we all agreed that we wanted to provide a diversity of Vetch memorabilia, but with absolutely no compromise on quality. The contents, therefore, offered another challenge – and in this, we were at times in danger of including too much.

We all agreed that we should cover the full media spectrum of sound, vision and the written and photographic record, with the emphasis firmly on the Vetch, its life, its environs and its memories, as opposed to another history on the trials and tribulations of Swansea City Football Club – the Vetch has far greater significance than as a football venue alone. The overriding principle was to think in terms of what the fans would want, and with the group predominantly made up of North Bankers, we always felt comfortable that we could achieve that aim. Of course, with an initial complement of seven, there were divergences of opinion in many areas, with frequent heated discussions, but the fact that we were all pursuing the one aim was always the determining factor that drove us forward.

Another prime consideration, and a potential obstacle, was securing the finance to fund the project. Hand in hand with this was the decision on how many box sets to produce. How many could we realistically expect to sell? How would we raise the funds to cover our set up, marketing and production costs? As is so often the case in South West Wales, corporate financial support was in short supply, so it quickly became apparent that we would need to be self-funding.

The box sets themselves were delayed in distribution because of our principles of presenting a quality product and our desire to include a 'piece of the Vetch' inside each box set. We were on the hunt for something meaningful, yet practical, retrievable and with the need to be able to obtain 1,000 of the same. We considered pieces of terracing, seat numbers and, of course, turf but they all had their practical problems.

After several visits to the Vetch and still in a quandary, it was suggested by Leigh Dineen that we consider looking in the area of the former Double Decker stand where, he believed, many parts of the original structure were still intact. To our surprise, contained within the new roof confines of the West Terrace, we found sections of the Double Decker stand and the staircases, not only still intact but in remarkably good condition. The end result was that we included a wood cutting from the Double Decker stand with a sepia coloured image of the stand on one side.

The Vetch box set was ready in late 2005 and, thanks to the work of the trust volunteers and others, a large number of the 1,000 produced were sold, in what we thought was a fitting and long lasting tribute to the Vetch as we moved homes. Over £30,000 in profit was made from the production and sale of these box sets with profits split evenly between the trust and the club, giving a big boost to the coffers of both with the trust share assisting with the future purchase of shares.

If the Ivor statue and the Vetch box set were resounding successes, our next project to celebrate our history may not have been one of our ideas, but as the trust took up the momentum as the driving force behind the project it was another huge credit to us when it came to fruition.

The concept behind the Robbie James bust came shortly after the stadium placed a bronze bust of John Charles in the entrance to the Liberty Stadium. Robbie's son, Luke, felt that as John had never played for the Swans then his dad should be commemorated as he explained,

As I've got older, I've started to think about my dad more. I'm coming to terms with it all now and something I would love to see would be some kind of memorial to my dad. People tell me what a legend he was and how Swansea fans used to chant his name. It would mean so much to me if there was a tribute to him at the Liberty Stadium.

When we saw Luke's comments, given our desire to want to celebrate our history at the new stadium, it seemed only fitting that we join in to help raise the money for that memorial, and we launched our campaign late in 2007.

As with the Ivor Allchurch fund, it did not take much for the donations to start flowing, and less than a month later we undertook a bucket collection at the Liberty Stadium prior to a Friday night game against Huddersfield. The memorial fund had a donation target of £6,000 and over £1,700 was collected that first night, as well as a donation of £500 being received from one donor, meaning that we were almost halfway towards our target. That bucket collection to me was a pivotal moment in realising just how much we do encompass and embrace our history. The collection took place the same night as Children in Need was on BBC TV, and often we were blanked as we waved the buckets at people, but the moment they realised what the collection was for they returned and placed money in the bucket with extreme generosity.

As online donations came in, we saw monies arrive from QPR and Cardiff fans among others, both clubs for which Robbie had played, and we realised that his legendary status went far beyond the Britton Ferry Bridge, which, added to another race night in early 2008, meant we surpassed the appeal target with some to spare.

The bust of Robbie James was unveiled – again outside the ticket office – in April 2008, having been sculpted by local sculptor Peter Nicholas. Once again, Swans fans turned up in their hundreds to witness the unveiling, along with many of Robbie's former teammates as well as members of his family. He, like Ivor, now looks out towards the Vetch.

When we had finished the fundraising for the Robbie James bust, there was some money left over, which we were determined to use for another tribute in Robbie's name. Our first idea was for a memorial garden behind the South Stand at the stadium. We have been aware that ashes are scattered at the stadium – my own brother's were scattered there after he passed away in September 2009 – but the area around Ivor's statue was bare and we discussed plans for sprucing up the area and making it more fitting for a memorial area for anyone who wanted to have their ashes scattered. However, for a variety of reasons we were struggling to get that idea off the ground so we moved on to a wall of fame. With our centenary year fast approaching, we felt that we had probably completed the busts and statues at the stadium, but recognised that there were many notable names in our past and future who were worthy of some form of commemoration at the stadium.

We discussed the idea with Robbie's family and they gave us the blessing for the Robbie James Wall of Fame, which was officially announced at the awards dinner held at the stadium in May 2011. The initial plan was to induct ten names a year for ten years, although in 2013 we changed that to be twenty names a year, with the last names being inducted and unveiled in 2016. The first twenty names were unveiled in 2012 and the next twenty will be unveiled in 2013. It was with pride that thirteen of the first twenty inductees were represented at the unveiling last year, and we hope for similar success in future years. The wall itself contains plaques of the players and managers who are being inducted into the Wall of Fame and they sit below the bust of Robbie, adding to his legacy at the football club.

The other notable event that we have commemorated within our history is that of the football club's centenary. Once again, as a trust we were keen to do our own marking of this event with a notable production that would capture 100 years of the Swans. This was a challenge for us, because we were very mindful that it was only seven years since we had undertaken the Vetch box set project, and we were very keen not to produce something that appeared to be made up of 'leftovers' from that project. The celebration of 100 years of a football club deserves more than that.

We teamed up with a great team of people from Swansea University – Phil Bethell, Martin Johnes and Huw Bowen – and were able to win a heritage lottery fund grant to assist with the project, which made life much easier as we could appoint a project manager to assist us with a massive amount of research for the books that were about to be produced.

The first book was released in July 2012 at the start of the centenary season and as we stated at the time:

> For 100 years people have followed the Swans. There have been good times and bad times. There have been moments of joy and despair. Players and managers have come and gone but the supporters are always there.

To celebrate the club's centenary, the supporters' trust has produced a book of fans' memories and stories. Packed with photographs from across the club's 100-year history, the book is a treat for any supporter. It contains contributions from fans of all ages, from schoolchildren to those who saw their first game in the 1920s. The stories are both funny and sad and reflect the club's colourful and sometimes turbulent history. It's a book about passion and commitment. It's about cheering in the stands and looking out for results on the other side of the world. It's about favourite spots on the terrace and strange superstitions. It's about family and friends. It's about why we care. It's about why we're 'Swansea 'til I die'.

Once again, we saw the book fly off the shelves and a second one is currently in publication after the success of the first. Again, we were driven by our determination to produce something that was high quality and worthy of celebrating such a great history as that of the Swans, rather than producing something quickly that maybe did not quite hit the spots that we would want it to.

In addition, thanks are due to the work of the guys at the university who pieced together a website that is now a fantastic archive of the Swans history and well worth a look if you haven't done so already (http://scfcheritage.wordpress.com/).

Although the commemoration of our history is not one of the primary objectives of the trust, I would argue strongly that some of this work is about bringing the club closer to the community, as we discussed in the last chapter. It is always pleasing to pass the statue, bust or wall of fame at the Liberty and remember the work that we put into getting it there, and this is something that I can only see continuing in the years to come, although we always have to be mindful that the stadium is not owned by the club, and therefore we have to learn to walk before we can run and talk to the stadium management about any plans.

However, the history of the club remains massively important to us, and our lifetime achievement award also contributes to celebrate this history. And within the commemoration of that history, we will always be grateful to all the fans that dig their hands in their pockets and have made these things possible.

11

Generosity

The manner of giving is worth more than the gift.
Pierre Corneille, 1606–84

Ask any person from any fundraising organisation and they will tell you that one of the greatest battles they face is the whole purpose of the organisation – finances. Almost naturally, as human beings, we are built the same and if someone waves a bucket or a donation form in front of you, the first instinct is almost always to turn away and look for an excuse not to donate rather than putting your hand in your pocket and parting with money.

Whether it be someone knocking on your front door, approaching you in the street or a letter dropping onto your doormat with the monthly bills, it is exceptionally hard to persuade people to part with their money. I do not write that as a criticism of people as I am no different, but it is an ongoing challenge for us as a supporters' trust and one that is now becoming harder for it.

However, I do believe that there is one thing that we have going for us as an organisation when we ask for money, and that is that the fans of a football club generally have more passion for their club than the ordinary Joe would in the street for a given charity. Of course that changes – for example you are more likely to want to support a cancer charity if you have lost a loved one to the disease – but it does feel different as a football club. Look back on the chapters around our early years at the trust and you have many examples of generosity from supporters.

Of course, in those early years we were a club in crisis. From a personal perspective, I will never forget the six months from July 2001 to January 2002 that I firmly believe galvanised this football club, and had the events of that period not happened, we would not be where we are now. I was not involved in the running of the trust back in that period, but I remember being on the North Bank and the Centre Stand and watching the bucket being passed around, and was amazed at how many people would put their hand in their pocket to donate to the cause.

The challenge for us now on the finance side is ensuring that we have enough money in our coffers to succeed in the aims of the trust. For the main part of our existence we have been cash rich, and that is obviously a good place to be. As already stated, the early days were relatively easy and money was raised in plentiful supply as people bought into the concept of owning part of their local football club. When the current owners took charge of the club we had around £30,000 towards the cause and the shareholders gave us extended time, to the end of March that year, to increase that shareholding to £50,000. By the end of 2003, we had over £80,000 invested and, with club finances at the time still in a fragile state, shareholders were asked to consider short-term loans to keep the club on track. These loans were translated into shares and that extended our shareholding to £100,000 after the move to the Liberty Stadium.

The final part of this investment was almost exclusively down to a piggyback scheme that was introduced in our last season at the Vetch and continued into the first season at the Liberty. This scheme meant that, as people were renewing (or buying) their season ticket, their membership fee was deducted from the amount the club received and this was used to purchase their membership of the trust. Fans had an 'opt out' option, but in the main people did not take this up and we had a large number of members as a result, but more importantly a very large share fund accumulating, which allowed us to continue building a shareholding with the club.

To our disappointment, the piggybacking ended for our second season in the Liberty, which hit us in the pocket, but acted to energise our efforts to keep the funds flowing in, which takes us back to the opening comments in this chapter. We have considered many schemes to increase numbers since that date, including regular and one-off donations, but the one thing we have been unable to do is a bucket collection. The club has progressed every season since we changed homes in 2005 and it just is not right to even try and claim that we need bucket collections to survive. Sure, we held one for the Robbie James fund, but beyond that we have not looked into it at all. This has clearly led to a reduction in our income over that time, but with the club on a stable footing we have not needed the income to support them and therefore the need for money has probably subsided, although clearly not disappeared completely.

As an organisation, we still believe in 'rainy days'. Most of us have been around long enough to remember previous periods of success at the club – the Toshack era immediately springs to mind – but they have always been followed by a darker period where things were not so good. I suspect that if you looked back to the late 1970s and early 1980s and asked fans at the time if they saw the rise ending then many of them would have answered with a resounding 'no'. Of course, football is a different animal these days, and through our careful management and principles at the club we are much more secure then we were then, but we do not believe that it will last forever. I guess what I am saying here is that our viewpoint has changed, in that the desire to raise money is not essential for this season or even next, but we are building a 'war chest' should we need it at some point in the future.

In the last twelve months, we have been helped significantly by the payment of two dividends by the club, which currently sees us sitting healthily with over £400,000 in our bank accounts. But if you think logically, £400,000, given the potential market value of a share in the club, is now possibly worth less than the £30,000 we invested back on day one of the current consortium, in terms of what it can buy. So our campaign to raise money continues.

Interestingly, we have had debates over the years about whether we should speculate to accumulate. There is a belief that if we used a sum of money to invest in a person to 'work' our database to raise money and awareness of the trust, that we may recoup that investment two- or threefold (or even more), but it is something we have not followed through on, although that is not to say that it will never happen. One of our fears is that we do not necessarily want to become one of those organisations that we almost naturally hang up on when we receive a call, but there is also the fear that we may not get back that investment, and we have to consider that when we are effectively playing with the money from our members.

As a trust, we have always been keen not to set expectations of our shareholding in the club. At the outset we had the aim that we wanted to have a shareholding, which we have achieved, but even as we grew as an organisation we never really wavered on this front. However, there was always a difference in view between fans and even trust board members on how much was a realistic aim for the trust and what was the 'ideal' position.

As Nigel Hamer explained to jackarmy.net late in 2003,

> We haven't set a target figure for our investment in the club; as and when funds become available and there are shares available to purchase, we shall invest, but our immediate aim will be to reach the £100,000 mark in the next few months.
>
> There are fans out there who would like to see the trust owning the club 100 per cent as has happened at York City, but having been close enough to the financial feedback that we get from our supporter director, I like to be able to sleep at nights! Seriously though, I would not wish to see this trust own much more than we currently do today, which is approximately 20 per cent. Having seen the work put in by the current board, I cannot envisage anyone having the time as well as earning a living, to be involved in running a football club under the guise of the supporters' trust.

I think Nigel had it spot on back then and I do not think that has changed at all. I do not believe we would have had the rise that we have if the trust had owned the club completely and, even now, although we have tens of millions coming in every year, I do not think complete ownership would ever be an option. Nigel's point is about the day-to-day running of the club and under trust ownership we would need to employ an army of people to do this – far more than we have now, given the work that all our directors perform. We remunerate some of them for that work, but it is still a fraction of what other clubs at our level spend, and we are more comfortable with it that way. The dream to own 100 per cent will likely remain just that. Although there are clearly examples where fan ownership does work, I am just not convinced it ever would for Swansea City.

So although we have no target figure for shareholding, we do retain a belief that we should hold over 10 per cent of the club, for the simple reason that it is the level where we cannot be forced to sell in the event of any takeover. And if we cannot be forced to sell, then we always have a director on the club board, and that remains extremely important to us.

If accumulating funds is hard work at times, another clear focus that we always have for the trust is in membership numbers. You may argue as to why we need to worry about membership numbers when we own such a considerable stake in the club, and it is a good question and one that we have debated many times as a trust board. Membership does not increase our shareholding or influence within the club, but we do have the belief that it gives us greater impact to talk about representing 5,000 members than 1,000. As with collecting money, it is substantially easier to talk people into becoming a member when the situation is dire than it is when things are going well. You can take reference in this statement from the fact that during our first year we had almost 1,500 members, but this dropped by around 30 per cent in the second season after the club had changed ownership. Thinking back to the launch meeting of the trust, people were ready to join and sign their names to become members because of the position of the club and the state of the ownership, but just twelve months later maybe the desire was not there.

Of course, you could always argue that people's hesitance to join the supporters' trust could be down to things that we do that maybe they do not agree with, but particularly in those early two years you would almost certainly put it down to reacting when there is an actual crisis and slipping back into apathy mode when there is no perceived crisis.

One of the catalysts that did boost our membership numbers after that initial couple of years was the piggybacking of the season tickets during the two years either side of our move to the Liberty. As the club started to sell more and more season tickets, we were able to get more numbers on our books, although we always continued with the debate of whether we were better with a smaller membership number who took the decision to join the trust, or was it more beneficial to have a higher membership number, but accept that some of them may have joined by default without actually realising what opting in was meaning to them. This is a debate that we still have now, and I do not think there is a right and a wrong answer to the question – it is just one that remains a point of debate with no real resolution.

As the piggybacking ended, membership numbers dropped again to what appears to be a standard for us of between 1,000 and 1,500. Although that is a small percentage of our average gate (even when we were in League One), I always took it as a positive that we had that kind of hard core that believed in us enough to want to join the trust, especially at a time when it was becoming more obvious that the team and the club was on the up. These people clearly believe enough in the trust organisation to want to give us the membership fee each year, and clearly see the benefit of what a strong supporters' trust can give them.

During these times, we used to have people out and about around the Liberty on a matchday trying to build up membership numbers, but it was a thankless task, as we needed time to talk to people to convince them of the reasons to join the trust, and this meant that we could probably only talk to maybe five or six people per matchday, which meant that membership growth was always going to be a slow process. To counter this, we produced a leaflet that outlined the reasons why people would want to consider joining the trust – we handed this out on matchdays to try and increase numbers, which helped a little, but reading a leaflet is probably not as effective as actually listening to someone explain the reasons, as strange as that may sound.

Around the start of 2011 we had a debate, as the trust approached its tenth birthday, about the value of membership. During those ten years we had offered membership discounts at local businesses and there was a time when trust membership would offer you priority on match ticket sales, but that was dwindling as more matches headed towards sell-outs, meaning less tickets were available for sale. So we took the decision that for 2011/12 we would go down a different route and offer free membership. This may have been seen as a strange decision given our desire for finances, but we had a plan that if we offered free membership then we could talk to the club again about making all season ticket holders trust members, which at the time we believed would give us around 7,000 members. Our plan then was to use effective communications with these fans to encourage regular donations into the trust, which would give us the same income as normal membership levels previously had. The plan was agreed by the club but then to our delight we had a stroke of luck (if you can call it luck) in that the team produced a push for promotion to the Premier League and the club started to maximise on that possibility by selling season tickets at Championship prices for what was looking like it could be a Premier League season. Ticket sales went through the five-figure barrier and way beyond after promotion was confirmed and we found ourselves with more than 13,000 members – our highest number ever. Such was the success of this scheme that we continued it in the second season in the Premier League with similar numbers of membership.

However, for this coming season (2013/14), we recognised that we needed to undertake a review of the membership and we have slightly adjusted the membership scheme again, to keep free membership but introduce a paid membership level as well which comes with voting rights. Voting rights are fundamental to us as a trust, as it can shape our future direction and while overall membership numbers are important, we also believe that if we wanted to gauge a membership opinion or put an important point out for discussion then having a core of people who fundamentally believe in what we do is extremely important. At the time of writing we are yet to see the effect of these membership changes, but we hope that it will give us around the 1,000–1,500 members that we previously had on the paid basis.

Going forward I do not know in which direction we will take membership numbers and levels, but I do believe that it remains important for us as an organisation to retain a high membership number that we can refer to should the club ever fall into hard times, and get messages across to people quickly if the need ever arose again which, ironically, we all hope never happens.

One of the opportunities that membership of the trust can bring is the chance to put yourself up for election to the main trust board, something that many have done over the years, determined to make a difference to the future of not just the trust but the club as well.

Much earlier in this book you would have seen many names crop up time and time again during our foundation as an organisation and the work done by many back in the period in the second half of 2001 should never be forgotten. Since then, the trust board has seen many faces come and go, all holding a variety of positions. For example, I am the fourth chairman of the trust following John Parkhouse, Leigh Dineen and Ron Knuszka in the role, and of course Leigh and Huw have both represented the trust at club board level. These are the two roles that become the figurehead roles of the organisation but behind these people are a group of hard-working individuals who put in many hours to ensure that the trust can grow. I look at the work that goes into our annual raffle or the bowling night, and it is many hours of labour that often go unnoticed at any time other than the Annual General Meeting, when I (or whoever is chair at that time) take the opportunity to thank our board members for their contribution.

Typically, the trust board will meet once a month at the Liberty for around two hours, although we have several sub-groups looking at aspects of the trust work that could mean sub-group meetings mid-month as well, as they prepare to report back to the trust board itself. At a typical board meeting we will hear the latest on our financial position and updates on what activities we have planned (be it a forum or a social event for example), together with an update from the supporter director on what is happening at club level. Much of the information we receive from the supporter director is confidential and therefore does not get recorded when we publish our minutes and I hope that our membership realises why this is the case. As a shareholder of the club, the trust board will receive this information, but cannot release any information that could be damaging to the club if it were in the public domain – as an example, transfer information could be part of this or even the financial position of the club. As a board, we need to respect the confidentiality of the information that we receive, although we also recognise that we owe our membership the right to be kept informed of anything that impacts on us as an organisation.

The volunteering aspect of the trust board becomes more vital to us when we are undertaking any form of social events. The biggest example for me is the annual awards dinner, which only comes about following around three months of biweekly meetings to discuss the various aspects of the dinner and ensuring that it is all completed within the timescales. This will involve looking for awards sponsors, collating nominations for the various awards, selling places at the dinner, securing raffle prizes and working hand-in-hand with the club and the stadium to ensure the evening is the success that it always is. And this is where we do not just rely on board members, for we always have people on hand for these events that will step in and assist us when we ask them. At this particular event we also work closely with our friends at the executive fundraising committee and the work and organisation of Steve McLelland, John Gregory and Ray Trotman is invaluable for this period as a fantastic evening is pieced together.

If it were not for this army of volunteers then these events would be nowhere near as successful as they are. It can be something simple like selling raffle tickets at the bowling night or collecting in money at the awards dinner, or something more like providing trophies or whiskey for the winners at the awards dinner, but all play a vital part in the trust cog that works at these events to run them so smoothly. Thankfully, as we have said before in this book, Swansea City is a very close-knit family and that runs right throughout our fan base, and we always count ourselves lucky as I am not sure that some of the help that we get could ever be replicated at clubs elsewhere. I think it is just typical of the way that this club has everybody behind it that people are only too willing to step in and help us out.

At this point, I think it is only fair to recollect something from the summer of 2011, when we first took our membership to around 13,000 thanks to those who joined the trust as season ticket holders. This presented us with a bigger logistical challenge than we have ever faced before as to how we sent our annual newsletter to that many people. I think it was at this point that I realised just how lucky we were with people volunteering, as an army of helpers stepped in and for over two days they filled the press room at the Liberty stuffing envelopes with newsletters, letters, donation forms, raffle tickets and badges before posting them to all our members. It was a joy to watch this happening and made me feel proud that people cared that much to give up so much time to assist in our organisation. At the heart of all of this was our board member Alan Lewis, who has spent many of the early years of his retirement running around organising trust activities and his organisation for this particular exercise saw it all go as smoothly as possible.

To me, the overall success of the trust is dependent on all this generosity that we have talked about in this chapter: generosity to provide us with money – be it through an event, a membership fee or a donation – together with the people who work to make the trust a success behind the scenes. We have thoroughly documented just what a success story the Swansea City Supporters' Trust is, but it would never have been possible without all these people.

12

Shareholding

Buy with your heart, not your head. You can look at all the aspects that make a purchase practical, but that kind of thinking makes it an investment rather than a home.

Barbara Corcoran, 1949–

I guess it is rare for anyone to purchase shares in any company with anything other than the thought in mind to turn a profit and make a return on any investment. Indeed, for many there is no other point in investment, but it has been said many times that football clubs are like no other business. Although many have believed that there is money to be made in a football club, which is potentially true, especially now with the revenues generated in the Premier League, but it certainly was not the case back in 2001 at our formation, or in 2002 when we first invested money into the football club.

However, while we were not investing for any profit, you also have to realise that Tony Petty, and Ninth Floor before him, thought that there was a profit to be made with investment in Swansea City, and you would probably assume that Mel Griffin and Bo Ekland also believed the same when they were considering an investment in the club. The difference with the shareholders group that we were part of back in 2002 was that we were investing to safeguard the future of the club and at that point certainly did not see that there was a profit to be earned. In truth, as a supporters' trust, our motives for investment were always about meeting our aim to have a shareholding in the club and retain it at a level that secured that shareholding as a percentage, and retained our place on the board of directors.

The shareholders' agreement that is currently in place states simply that if we retain a 5 per cent shareholding in the club then we are entitled to a seat on the board of directors. This is a fantastic safeguard for us as an organisation, and I believe that it is a wonderful protection for the club going forward as well, as I firmly believe that a voice – no matter how quiet – is better than no voice at all.

And it was the dream of having a shareholding in the club that drove much of our early success, as this seemed to be something that people latched onto as an ambition that we could achieve in the long run, although as we have seen the long run quickly turned into the short term! And it was not just the ordinary fan in the street that was latching onto this dream; Mel Nurse was also right behind it as he said in a statement not long after Tony Petty arrived in Swansea:

> Support the supporters' trust. They will be a big player in the overall picture and the future of our club. To those of you who haven't joined the trust, I appeal to you to join today. To those of you who have, please consider increasing your donations to their share fund.

Mel was, of course, a driving force behind the consortium that took control in that early part of 2002. He has also been a long-serving supporter of us as a consortium and it was a remarkable act of generosity on his behalf when, towards the end of 2009, he donated all proceeds from his book, *Mel Nurse – Mr Swansea*, to the trust. At the time, Mel commented, 'Directors, players and managers come and go. But there is one thing that is constant and that is the supporters. This cheque is to help towards the continuing good work the trust do on behalf of the supporters.' And when we have people like Mel backing our work and urging people to contribute to the share fund, then our work becomes just a little bit easier.

As a trust we currently have invested in the football club a grand total of £199,999. This represented for a long time an investment of 19.99 per cent in the football club, but in the last couple of years this has effectively become a 21 per cent investment, after the club purchased back shares from Mel Nurse, which reduced the issued share capital from £1 million to £950,000. We remain the joint second biggest shareholder in the football club behind Martin Morgan, who owns 23.6 per cent and level with Brian Katzen, who has the same shareholding as us at the trust. I think when you look at the numbers and values of what has been invested, then it is incredible to think that we worked ourselves in to a position to invest that kind of money as an organisation.

As you can imagine, though, that investment did not come about in one particular tranche of investment. The aim when the consortium came about was to invest £50,000 into the club to secure that shareholding, although when the deal was actually signed to take control of the club we only had £30,000 available to us. The gap was, of course, closed very quickly by the generosity of Gareth Keen, who donated his shares to us, and we were able to secure the further £10,000 that we needed to give us the investment that we wanted by the deadline date.

The £50,000 turned to £100,000 over an eighteen-month period between February 2003 and August 2004, thanks to some of the schemes that we had in place at the time, although it was mainly the loan schemes that allowed us to increase our shareholding in the club. This was not universally popular with other shareholders, but it was something that was afforded to us as an organisation and we will always be grateful for that opportunity to increase our shareholding. At this point, we were running on par with a 20 per cent shareholding in the club, which was possibly more than we had ever dreamed of, and as the club won promotion from League Two and moved home from the Vetch to the Liberty, as an organisation we were in an exceptionally strong position. The club was finally on the up and we had more than played our part in less than four years from formation.

Not long after the move to the Liberty Stadium, there was some discussion at our monthly board meetings around loans made to the club back in the darker days by some of the shareholders. These loans had never been repaid by the club and there was now some debate between shareholders as to whether the loans could be converted into shares, with a release of extra share capital from the level of £500,000 and taking it up to £1 million for the first time since the new owners had moved into place. Eventually it was agreed that the loans could be converted into shares, and that gave us a new dilemma in how to get money into our coffers to raise our own shareholding within the club. Without new investment for us, it would mean a share of 20 per cent diluting down to just 10 per cent which, although still significant, was lower than the ideal level that we wanted.

It was time to go public again, and so we released the following statement where I appealed to our members, and Swans fans everywhere, for more money for our share fund. The statement read,

It has been over five years since the supporters' trust played a huge role in the ousting of Tony Petty and the return of the club to the fans. It is an achievement of which we are rightly proud and we are also proud of the part that we have played in the club moving forward from that position to the position of today, where we challenge for promotion to the Championship in front of five-figure crowds at our new stadium. Some progress in a five-year period! Our contribution has been sizeable in terms of input via our two supporter directors during that time, as well as organisation of numerous events that have brought the club closer to its supporters.

The club is now unrecognisable from the one that stood in January 2002 and, through the work of the shareholders and directors (of which we are an integral part), we have a club that many look up to as a benchmark of what can be achieved and what is possible even when it seems all is lost, as it probably did back in late 2001. It has not all been plain sailing of course – there was the flirt with the Conference in 2003 and further financial worries in the early years of the current set-up.

The club was nursed through those financial worries by the generosity of some of our shareholders, who loaned the club money to meet its running costs and ensure a continuation of trade. Perhaps not huge sums, but not loose change either, and the trust are extremely grateful to those that dug deep in their pockets to help sustain our club. Now, as a result of the agreement of all shareholders, these loans are to be converted into shares in Swansea City. As a trust, we feel it only right to agree that the sums introduced in these circumstances be recognised as investment monies.

All other shareholders have been given the chance to increase their stakes accordingly, and as a supporters' trust we are no different. We have been given the opportunity to double our existing shareholding of £100,000 and because of the nature of the makeup of our organisation we have been given an extra period to raise this money. We have a figure of £60,000 already put aside for this purpose and, acting on the mandate given to us by our members, we will be handing this to the club in return for shares. That means a minimum stake of 16 per cent in Swansea City Football Club, and if we raise a further £40,000 then that shareholding will increase to 20 per cent, owned by us, the fans.

In addition, we have given our backing, along with that of the other shareholders, to increase the authorised share capital of the club from £1 million to £2 million. This does not mean an immediate injection of £1 million into the club, but it means that the club can issue extra shares to that value at a time when the business needs the investment. Again, as a trust, we will be given the chance each and every time to subscribe to these shares to maintain our shareholding percentage. It is definitely worth remembering here that we will be given longer timescales, because of the nature of our makeup, to raise any additional funds on further share issues.

And it is now that we have to pass things over to you, as supporters, to make your decisions as to what we should do from here on in. Let me share some facts with you:

Irrespective of whether we invest above the £60,000 we immediately intend to deposit, our director's place on the club board is not in jeopardy. The club board operates on crucial decisions on a 'one vote per director' basis – certain issues outside of the day-to-day running of the club are influenced by percentage ownerships. All shareholders with a 5 per cent shareholding have been invited to have a director on the board. Even if, at some stage in the future, our shareholding dropped below 5 per cent then we would retain a directors position. Please never underestimate the value of this – the director is involved in *all* major decisions the club undertakes.

It is a magnificent testament to the work of the current directors, including the trust director, that successful businessmen are prepared to invest further in a club that less than four years ago could have become a non-League club.

The supporters' trust are committed to ensuring that safeguards are put in place to ensure that all monies are used for the greater good of the football club, and will advocate the preparation of detailed financial plans in respect of all future investment proposals. Success on the pitch is something we all want to share, but at no stage must the club's future be gambled on chasing that dream.

The release of a further £1 million of share capital will allow the club to continue its successful development, and increasing the share capital is a preferred option to taking on bank borrowings.

Every time the club board vote to release more shares, we will be given the option to subscribe to that share issue.

The supporters' trust has been given a clear message in the past by its supporters that it should be concentrating in the main on its shareholding within the club. This is something that is only achieved by further investment within the trust, which in turn goes to the club.

It is now time to decide, as supporters, whether you want the shareholding to remain constant or whether you are prepared to let that figure reduce as other shareholders gain larger shareholdings. It is a question that only you can answer for yourself – on this subject I really cannot influence you.

I now ask you to consider the requirements of us maintaining our shareholding:

SHORT TERM
£40,000 investment in the trust. We currently have several events planned and with membership fees for next season then maybe we could secure £10–20,000 of that. That leaves £20–30,000 to find, which can only come from increased memberships, lump sum donations or substantial savings on a regular monthly basis. If you want us to maintain our shareholding then please consider at least one of those three. Every little helps towards that target.

LONG TERM
We would envisage that further share issues will take place in the future. We therefore need to consider a turnover on trust funds in excess of £100,000 per year. This will be achieved through

membership fees, one-off donations or regular donations into trust coffers. Again, if you wish us to continue to buy shares in the club then please consider at least one of these three. In addition to these ideas, we are also looking into the possibility of fans being able to bequeath money to the trust – we will keep you informed on this front.

This is a crossroads for the supporters' trust. We are firmly committed to play our part in moving the club forward, and we expect to play a very big part in that progression. We are delighted to see our new director integrate seamlessly into the club and continue the work of his predecessor, and we know that we are involved in every major decision that the club takes. We are also pleased to say again that the director position is not under any threat, short term or long term, and supporters should take comfort in that fact.

A larger shareholding gives us an increased chance to veto any future Tony Petty type characters who may eye up the club as a 'cash cow'. Your trust board firmly supports the idea of maintaining the supporters' shareholding as close to 20 per cent as possible, as has been indicated by our current membership. Despite the influence that comes through our seat on the board it is the shareholding that is of paramount importance in maintaining our influence in the long term. However, the ball is in your court as it is only through contributions and donations from our members that the trust will be able to sustain its present level of shareholding.

I apologise for having gone into such detail but, as a trust board, we feel that it is essential that I do just that and paint as full a picture as possible as to where we stand, the future plans of the club, and where we can progress from here.

It was a long statement, but one that we felt was appropriate, with the key for us possibly being the crossroads statement. As a board, we were aware at the time that the club was on the up, and this was a chance for people to decide just how much a significant shareholding in the club meant to them. £60,000 had come to us through two seasons of piggybacking on to the season tickets, but we were not to be afforded the luxury to gain the remainder via the same method. The other shareholders had been kind enough to give us more time to purchase shares, but we were also aware that if we did not get to the thresholds we needed, then others could snap up the rights to buy our shares.

The £60,000 was paid across to the club shortly after the release of our statement, but the raising of the last £40,000 was to take some time and did not come through as quickly as we had hoped when we released the statement. Thankfully, though, by this time we had become reasonably slick on our events calendar and between membership fees, the bowling night, annual raffle and awards dinners we had a reasonable income coming through each year and we were able to use this to fund some of the share purchases. A further £10,000 was handed over before May 2008 and another £20,000 by May 2009 that took our shareholding to £190,000 and, through our membership fees for the 2009/10 season, we managed to find the last remaining monies needed to take our shareholding to £199,999 or 19.99 per cent of the club.

In hindsight, although it took over two years to raise the money, when you consider the set-up we work with, and the fact that there is not one big donation among the last money raised, then it was an impressive feat to raise that kind of money off the back of ordinary events, and it meant that we retained the percentage shareholding that we craved.

You will recall from the statement when we were looking to raise money that the shareholders had voted to be able to raise the share capital of the club by £2 million. As we invested the last part of the current investment, our thoughts almost immediately turned to preparing a fund that would prepare us for the day when the increased share capital would be called upon. However, as the club progressed on the field then promotion to the Premier League overtook the need for the increase in share capital. Or at least it did for the time being.

As an organisation, we always have to be aware that this is a possibility that we may need to face, although the longer we spend in the multi-million-pound environment that the Premier League is, the further away that day appears to be. Of course the payment of two dividends in return for our shareholding has given us a very healthy fighting fund, and the mandate remains there from our members that our number one aim should be for shares in the club, so we sit on the large proportion of the money should we ever need it.

In the run up to the Capital One Cup final, there was a brief discussion on Sky Sports News around how much our 20 per cent shareholding was worth, and it was estimated that it could be worth £10 million, which is phenomenal for us as an organisation and highlights again what a remarkable story ours really is. Of course, with a valuation of that level then a fighting fund that contains around £400,000 may not stretch very far, but up and down the country there would be trusts queuing up to be in our position and it is one of which we are extremely proud.

As stated at the start of this chapter, we now own over 21 per cent of the issued shares of the football club, making us unique in Premier League terms, and all of that has been raised through donations from our members and the generosity of people like Mel and Gareth.

The final point of note to consider on shareholding is around minimum percentages that we would like to maintain. A key number for me is to maintain a 10 per cent shareholding. This remains important as it is the level of shareholding at which we can never be forced to sell. Therefore we retain our stake in the club and, most importantly, our representation on the board. The good news for me is that even if we did get to the stage where the share capital was doubled (as per the agreement) then we retain a 10 per cent plus shareholding so we have that safeguard for quite some period of time.

We definitely find ourselves, therefore, in a strong position on shareholding, not just for now, but should there be any future changes, and that can only be good, both for us as an organisation and for Swansea fans everywhere.

13

Communication

The great thing is to know when to speak and when to keep quiet.
Seneca the Younger, 4BC–AD65

One of the challenges that any supporters' trust has is to ensure that it remains at the forefront of the thoughts of the supporters of the club in which it has an interest. We have often said at the Swans Trust that our job is very easy when there is a crisis on the horizon or something is going wrong at the club, purely because that is when people look to us to be able to do something. It does not have to be Armageddon-type events like those that were taking place when we were formed, but it can be something simple like an increase in ticket prices. However, when everything seems to be going well, as it has done at Swansea for all of ten years, then it is a real battle for us as a trust to get people to understand why they would want to be members and, even more importantly now, why we would need a strong trust, when the football club turns over somewhere in the region of £100 million per year.

We have always been lucky with media coverage in that in the early days there was always a story about the trust and generally it was positive. Because we found ourselves at the forefront of the battle to regain control of the club, the media were always happy to speak to the trust about what was trying to be achieved, and this was even more evident to me when we started to piece together this book, as there was plenty of material to work within the archives of the various websites that I could use for research purposes.

The battle for the trust in those early days was to become known in the various media outlets as the voice of the fans. For a few years the media had grown used to a handful of contacts for media views. I was one as the publisher of jackarmy.net and there was Gary Martin at the time at scfc.co.uk, while you also found that Ugo Vallario or Keith Haynes were often quoted as the various heads of their supporters' groups (FOSCFA and MAGS respectively).

Particularly in those early days, it was Leigh Dineen and Marilyn Croft who were the voices of the trust, and Leigh in particular was very vocal in the trust press releases over happenings at the Vetch at the time. This lifted the profile of the trust in a way that benefitted us greatly. One of the early battles for us was won this year as the local media – club website included – was only too happy to publicise the happenings at the trust, and this was vital when you consider the early meetings that were necessary to get people to join up as members. Of course, we were helped by the actions of those who were in charge of the club in the early days, but we were growing our profile very quickly and very productively at the same time. Dave Boyle recognised this when I spoke to him, and he acknowledged that people outside of their work and family commitments were carrying out their (trust) duties as well, and in contrast with people who had much bigger media power at their disposal. Here he was referring to the fact that those in charge of the club had a media department (although notably at the time Swansea's media department was one man!) and access to the press as and when they wanted it.

If you think back to the start of this book, we talked about the Internet and the way that it changed how people viewed the Swans (off the pitch), and this was very much a medium that the trust used to our advantage in those early days. Swansea City had been very slow to grasp the Internet bubble that was building and the official site was a late addition to the Internet world; this had allowed two unofficial sites to steal a march in terms of securing visitor loyalty, and this meant that, despite the club having access to more media outlets, it was the trust who were able to gain a quicker and more effective audience through the sites at jackarmy.net and scfc.co.uk. Both sites supported the trust in terms of wanting to carry and publicise the news and even more so in the battle against Petty (or as it became known The War Against Tony – think about it!). It was these sites that were carrying the view of those that wanted control of the club long before the current incumbents of that ownership could even think about making their views known.

So in those early days, communication came really easily to the trust, and allowed us to gain a profile and standing within the support that quickly recognised us as the point of contact between club, media and fans. The second challenge comes from getting across the difference between what we do as a trust and what recognised supporters' clubs do. The easiest way to explain this cold to anyone is that, as a trust, we are simply the voice of the fans in the ear of the club. That is not to say that we will always be able to get the exact right deal for everyone (ticket prices would be a classic example of this), but we should be there to represent the interests of the fans in those discussions. What we, and all our members, need to remember is that the football club is run as a democracy on decisions. So while we can sit there and represent the fan views, we can easily be outvoted by our other directors, which can then give the impression that we have failed in one of our aims as a trust in not getting fans the best deal. However, as a shareholder of the club with our own director, we also have to make sure that we hit the right compromise between this and the commercial needs of the club.

Let me try and give you an example of this. During our first season in the Premier League, the discussion point arose around the renewal of season tickets for the following season. This discussion point arose early in the season and the view of the board (including our supporter director) was that if we brought forward the renewal date then season ticket sales would be maximised. The logic in this discussion was that if we were still in the Premier League, season ticket sales would exceed 15,000. If we were in the Championship it could be around half that. Asking for a renewal before the following season's status was known would help season ticket sales. The initial date was not well received by the fans and we were able to negotiate an extension to that date. This was always a tough one for us because we have to balance, as mentioned between the club's need to be commercially astute and ensuring that the fans are not completely trodden over. We felt we got the balance right on this occasion, which was backed by ticket sales in advance of the cut off dates. We appreciate at this point that it is never an ideal situation and in a perfect world we would probably have preferred not to have had to make the decision, but the difference in ticket sales for the club of around 7,000 is too much of a difference to just ignore if you work the maths through (around £2.5 million), which may have been revenue we would never have recovered had we left things the way that they were and had seen the team relegated. For us, it is a case of keeping the views of the fans in the ears of the club which, whether you agree with all decisions or not, is a luxury not afforded to all supporters of all clubs and that is important.

There are also other occasions when we may lose the 'battle', but what you won't find from us is a public washing of the reasons behind that. What we tend to do is just lick our wounds and come back and try again another day. A good example of this would be the piggybacking scheme that we had in place when we first moved to the Liberty. The scheme meant that we had all season ticket holders effectively as members of the trust. This was stopped after one season at the Liberty, which disappointed us, as it had given us a good income stream and a strong membership number. We continued to revisit this as an opportunity and eventually we got season ticket holders back as trust members when we reached the Premier League, which shows that it is good to never give up.

Soon after the current board took control of the club, a change in the way that we communicated to members commenced. In February 2002, we launched our first newsletter, which was four pages long. There is nothing new in using newsletters as a form of communication, but to most of our members at the time it was the first time they would have had a communication of this sort from anyone who was a part owner of the club. The initial aim with the newsletter was to produce four a season to send to all trust members, although in recent years – given the extensive cost that undertaking a mailing to 13,000+ members takes – we are down to just one printed communication per year, although it is worth noting that this communication now stretches to eight pages and beyond.

Interestingly, in that first newsletter, we were already looking at ways of increasing communication with members, as Paul Morris, board member at the time, explains:

As a trust, we have members throughout the UK and that's great. What isn't so great is the fact that it's sometimes very difficult to keep everybody informed of things that are happening on a fairly regular basis.

The newsletters will become a regular feature that will remedy most of the problem, but we would prefer to have some other line of information as well. That's where you all come in. We're looking for members who are interested in becoming 'points of contact' throughout the country and who can help relay information to other members in their 'area' and act as a go between with the Board and other Swansea-based committees or groups.

It was an idea that we have several times looked to explore, but as with any group that works on a purely voluntary basis it is always a challenge getting people to be able to combine all of this around their other commitments away from the trust.

As I mentioned before, communication in those first couple of years was relatively simple for us as a trust, but as circumstances changed and the club won promotion from League Two and moved to the Liberty Stadium there seemed to be in the eyes of many much less need for a strong supporters' trust. When you think that crowds had risen from around 3,000 at our formation to around four times that, there were many that wondered if the trust had run its course. For those of us that were working hard on the trust board, this was not seen as an insult but a demanding challenge to overcome. The challenge was doubled with the move to the Liberty. At the Vetch we had a trust HQ behind the North Bank, which at least gave us a point of focus and somewhere where we could meet people on a matchday. In truth it was a ramshackle old room that probably should have been condemned many years previously, but it was our room and somewhere we could call home. The new stadium did not afford us that luxury. We did have a presence in the club shop on a matchday, but in truth it was not the same and added to our challenge. When you also consider that an increase of average support by about 9,000 meant there were many who were not regular in the real bad times, and therefore potentially had no idea about what campaigns had already been won with the help of the trust, and who also had no real experience of the Swans in the down times. On the pitch, things were going well and back-to-back promotion was becoming a real possibility. We had 'foot soldiers' on the ground on a matchday, but in truth they could only hit so many people in the period of time available, and it was becoming harder to convince people of the benefits of a strong supporters' trust.

In that first season at the Liberty we had a 'piggybacking' of the season ticket scheme in that, unless people opted out of the scheme, £5 of the cost of their season ticket would be given to the trust in return for that season ticket holder becoming a trust member. This gave us a strong membership at around 5,000 and we tried to communicate with them via the newsletters, but when the piggybacking ended for the second season it became clear that the communication had not worked and renewals for many of them just never happened.

There were times when you almost wished for a mini-crisis to be able to latch onto in terms of something that we could work with. The club had money so did not need the bucket-type collections that had proved so successful in the past, and on the pitch we were experiencing success as the club picked up silverware at the Millennium Stadium before suffering play-off heartache just a month or so later.

The people in the ticket office helped us and we had leaflets on display in there, and we tried to highlight to people just how quickly fortunes could change in football – reinforced perfectly by a bright yellow leaflet we gave out at matches in 2008, which brought to people's attention the plight of Leeds United, who were with us in League One that season.

The leaflet read,

2nd May 2001 – European Cup Semi Final First Leg – Leeds United *v*. Valencia.

3rd May 2008 – Coca Cola League One – Leeds United *v*. Gillingham.

It can happen to anyone at anytime with little warning.

When Leeds drew with Valencia in that European semi-final first leg few would have envisaged seven years later they would ply their trade in the third tier of English football and start the season with a FIFTEEN POINT penalty.

And also remember that when you watched that match on TV you had never heard of Tony Petty – more evidence of how quickly things can turn.

This is proof if anyone needed it that the fortunes of a football club can change at any moment and a real reason to renew your membership of Swans Trust.

I do not really know whether any of these leaflets we handed out for a couple of games had any effect, but it seemed to be a logical approach to try and get people to take a viewpoint that although things were going well at that period of time (we had just won promotion to the Championship), it could change without warning. If people want examples of that now, you only have to look at events at Portsmouth, Hearts or Coventry as examples of how quickly the good times can turn into bad.

The one thing we always felt we missed, though, as a trust was something that people could take away and read to understand exactly what the trust was about and what the benefits were of having this in place for the fans. It was for this reason that we produced a trifold leaflet shortly after that, which detailed the benefits of the trust but also explained to people why they should consider being a member. With a Championship football club pushing on at the top end of that division and our support numbers growing again, we established that it was not practicable to provide anything other than a supply of these leaflets to hand out at games or to leave at the stadium for people to take away and read.

The leaflet read,

We believe that we are experiencing these good times because of the collective body of Swans fans at board level, of which the supporters' trust plays a major part. Should we ever fall on hard times again or be tempted to sell out to some foreign based millionaire then we need to be ready to act and ensure that the club does not repeat the mistakes of the past. Let us enjoy the good times but also be ready if things start going wrong by maintaining a significant shareholding.

We can only do that with your support and I urge you to consider joining the trust and becoming part of one of the biggest supporters' trusts in the UK. As chairman of the trust I promise you that I, and my fellow board members, will do as much as we can to ensure that your views are represented within the four walls of the Liberty Stadium, and that everything we do will be with the best interests of the club at heart.

It is hard to gauge whether this leaflet actually worked for us, but we know that supplies were dwindling and we managed to get some new members and regular donations, so we would like to believe that it made a difference and helped in some way.

The other significant form of communication that we have tried to grow is through our e-communications. We are fortunate at Swans Trust that we have a board member, Jim White, who runs his own CRM business and this has given us access to a sophisticated database management system that we are trying to use to our advantage. Having a system like this has given us the ability to send communications on a more frequent basis to our membership – or at least those that we have email addresses for – and also to mark against those that attend some of our social events to ensure that they are first to hear of future events. We have also used it on some of our fans' forum events, to inform people who live in the vicinity of the areas rather than blanket emails that hit people who could not possibly attend events outside of their area. This is still an area that we believe we can improve on greatly, but since we took our membership level to around 13,000 it has become a system that we have started to rely on, given the considerable costs that would be associated with communication via non-electronic methods.

Finally, the advent of social media outlets has also helped us greatly. The trust has both Facebook and Twitter pages alongside our website, and this means that we can get messages out into the world via these methods very quickly. We have gained over 2,500 followers on Twitter and regularly put our information out that way around social events, trust updates and anything that we think would be of interest to our followers.

Communication has come a long way since we launched the trust, and if we are being totally honest I am still not convinced that we are as good at it as we could be. However, what we have to maintain is a presence among supporters that is visible should the trust ever be needed to come to the aid of the club again. As we have seen with other examples, the security of any club is not guaranteed and while at the moment times are brilliant, as Swans fans we know that bad times can be just around the corner, as they have been before. What we aim to do at the trust is to keep that presence that I have talked about, so that if and when the crisis ever strikes our fan base will know where to turn to for the help that we will always be offering.

A benefit that we do appreciate, given our shareholding and input into the club, is the increased media presence, which is looked at in the next chapter of this book. This has greatly increased as the club has progressed and we have very much become the media darlings as far as supporters' trusts go, and to Supporters Direct we are their flagship model and the outlet that proves that supporters' trusts have a place in modern football and that input in to the clubs can be gained. Arguably, this level of media coverage is the best type that we can get, because it is gained off the back of other people recognising the work of the trust within the club, and that in itself generates a level of communication that reaches far wider than anything that we could produce ourselves.

14

Media

The idea that the media is there to educate us or to inform us is ridiculous because that's about tenth or eleventh on their list.

Sir Johannes Bjelke-Petersen

It is fair to say that the way the media has viewed us has changed out of all recognition since May 2011, when all of a sudden everyone wanted to know everything there was to know about Swansea City.

We have always had a good media presence, but mainly through the local media rather than anything nationally, other than the coverage that we got through the work of other supporters' trusts. The *Evening Post* used to give us a trust page on a regular basis, while the *Western Mail*, Swansea Sound and Real Radio have always been supportive of the work done by the supporters' trust.

As I mentioned in the last chapter, our media coverage in the early days was excellent. At times it seemed that a day did not pass where there was not a reference to the supporters' trust somewhere in the battle against Petty. Because of the breaking news that was constantly coming from the club, the trust were very active in their press releases and that gave us some immediate coverage that was well received in those early days.

However, outside of Swansea not much attention was really being paid to events that were happening here. You have to remember that we were a football club that plied their trade in the bottom division, and outside of a two-year jaunt into the top division, for the bulk of our eighty-nine-year history we had achieved very little. For the large part of our 'golden years' period under John Toshack, there was very little football coverage outside of the weekly edition of *Match of the Day*. Football became more of a media interest sport after the World Cup in Italy in 1990, while the advent of Sky Television and the growth in global demand for Premier League football did not take off until the mid-1990s, by which time it seemed that our best years were behind us, and to many media outlets there was not any worthwhile football that took place outside of the aforementioned Premier League.

So events at Swansea City were one of football's best kept secrets. It went very much unnoticed that we had gained a 20 per cent stake in our local football club, and that secured us a presence on the board for an ordinary fan, who was elected to represent the interests of all other fans at that board level. On the pitch, the football world seemed to also be ignoring that some of the football we were playing was going against the grain, and bringing a very different approach to the way the game was being played. Of course, there were brief moments where people stood up and paid attention. I distinctly remember a 1-1 draw with Fulham in the FA Cup in 2009 when Alan Green declared on Five Live after the game, 'I learned today that Swansea City played a beautiful brand of football. Please can we have them in the Premier League.' But these moments were few and far between and we were remaining an unknown quantity both on and off the pitch.

I always raised a smile when I read comments elsewhere that to succeed in the game you had to have a bottomless pit of money or a stadium that could house 50,000 people. We could see from our role within the club that we had developed a business model that worked perfectly off the pitch and that we had found the people on the pitch who could deliver the football that our fans wanted to watch. It was therefore quite irritating to us at the trust that we could not get this message through in the media, and that was not only an issue nationally but was also becoming one locally. For, despite the fact that the club was posting some pretty remarkable results on and off the pitch, the local media would focus more on events on the pitch backing up the theory that I mentioned before in this book, that our job as a trust is much easier when there is a crisis happening at the club rather than when things are going well.

As the club pushed on in the Championship, the dream of Premier League football coming to South Wales was becoming stronger. There were still trust mentions in the local press, but that was mainly down to wanting a comment over an event or an upcoming match, even in the weeks leading up to the play-off final in 2011. The club was clearly attracting more media coverage and that automatically gave us an increased media presence but focus, not surprisingly, was more about thoughts and hopes for the upcoming big game than the business model and club set-up that had become the catalyst for that success. In a way, that was no change to what we had experienced for around seven or eight years since the club reached a level of stability, but I do not think any of us expected that things were about to totally change, not just on the pitch but in the way that the outside world viewed the story that was Swansea City.

I do not need to explain to any Swansea fan the joy experienced on that day at Wembley, and the post-match celebrations, but it was the day after the play-off final that I think we at the trust realised that our presence was about to rise in the same way that the club's was. Our media guys spent most of the day after the play-off final at the Liberty Stadium, and were inundated with requests for information not just about the game the day before but about the club. It seemed that the world was waking up to Swansea City now that we were in the top flight, and this amazing story was generating increasing interest, not just about what Brendan Rodgers and his team had achieved on the pitch.

Trust media officer Alan Lewis takes up the tale:

It was probably fair to say that in the twelve months since the play-off final, the supporters' trust were more in the media spotlight than at any time since its origins back in the dark days of 2001. Then it was all about the survival of the club. Now we have journalists and reporters from all over the world keen to find out more about our football club.

The period immediately after our Wembley success was understandably one that saw the likes of Sky and other media outlets virtually camped outside the Liberty. It was as the season got underway, however, that the enormity of promotion into the Premier League began to sink in.

First it was a session with Eurosport and shortly after a crew from Norway's TV2 were in town. A couple of games into the season saw a request from Al Jazeera TV and it did not stop there. Japanese and German TV crews were followed by a journalist from the top French sports magazine *L'Equipe*. Fox News in both America and Australia also wanted to know more and the UK media was also taking more interest and articles about the trust appeared in most of the nationals.

This was an incredible phenomenon to us at the trust. And when you consider some of what was being said, the work that we had been part of at Swansea was being held up worldwide as the right way of doing things. That seemed strange to us, because as a trust we did not know any different as we had worked with it as a model through the club for all bar around six months of our existence.

SI.com wrote at the time,

> It is stories such as Swansea's that will give comfort to the several British clubs currently teetering like 2 a.m. drunks on a curb. Having been relegated to Division Three in 2001, the club twice changed hands for £1 – less than a dollar fifty – before a group of businessmen and supporters were able to start making plans a decade ago.

And this kind of comment was typical of the responses that we were getting. It seemed amazing that nobody had previously picked up on the story that we had watched develop in front of our own eyes. Maybe it was partly our fault as an organisation that we did not beat the drum loud enough or maybe we were happy slipping under the radar at the time, but it certainly caught us by surprise just how many people were amazed at the story when it climaxed in the ultimate promotion to the Premier League.

In fairness, there was one journalist who had always given us good publicity and that was David Conn from the *Guardian*. David is a football fan through and through and had always highlighted the good work that was being done at Swansea. David has written many column inches around finances in football and has always backed the model that we work with, and the results that we have achieved as a result of it.

These articles from David did not just cover our period of promotion to the Premier League, as he had always been a supporter of the way that we set about things at Swansea, and would always mention it in a positive light, so it was no surprise when he wrote in April 2012,

> The Swans' is one of modern football's most remarkable rises. In an English League that has placed faith for its club's futures in the hands of absentee billionaires, Swansea have become the first club, in the Premier League's twentieth season, with an elected supporter serving as a director on the board: Huw Cooze.

The article was very much focused around the trust and our shareholding in the club, and I believe it is simply the most positive piece of journalism that we have received in our eleven-year history, and highlights that the trust is an equal partner in the way the club is run.

Maybe we were naïve, but we believed that when we received our dividend from the club David would talk positively about the payment given the rags-to-riches story of the club and the trust. We knew we had a supporter in a well-respected journalist and we wanted to see how he would greet the news. However, we were disappointed when we read the article that appeared under the headline that 'Swansea City's halo slips as owners decide to pocket £2m windfall'. In fairness to David, he did not really hammer us as a trust for the decision, but he had spoken to Huw Jenkins, which was against our wishes in us giving him the heads-up. David wrote at the end of the article, 'Swansea City had seemed to embody the former ethos, a beaming exception, and now, with this dividend, that has changed. Except for the supporters' trust, which holds its shares as a mutual body, still for not pay, just for the committed sense of belonging.'

None of this is to say that David is now no longer a believer in the trust or the work that we have done at Swansea, but it is disappointing to see that he had used none of the information that we had given him about how positive this payment was for the trust, but had gone about the article with a different approach, which potentially could have caused us problems in our relationship with the club. From our side it was a learning exercise and maybe a mistake that we will not repeat, but nonetheless it was a disappointing moment for us.

One of the most interesting instances of media coverage we have had is a piece that we submitted to Parliament as part of the governance report on ownership of football clubs. In the report (January 2011), we highlighted the work that we had done to gain back control of the club, and emphasised some of the key things that we have done since we gained our shareholding to improve the relationship between club and fans. The report said in summary,

> Without the work of the supporters' trust there may well have not been a football club at Swansea City if it was not for the work that went in to save our club. Critically now, following that crisis, the supporters and the community have a voice in the way the club operates, which adds to that feeling of togetherness and trust that seems to be lacking with most other clubs where fans are purely treated as customers. We add a lot more than money to the club, be it professional skills, a unique understanding of our heritage and community, volunteer time, check and balance to the financial strategy, or two-way communication between the fans and the board.
>
> From our own experience at Swansea we would urge the committee to look to ways they can facilitate meaningful supporter involvement like ours at other clubs, including where a privately owned club fails to explore legislation that enables a new club to be owned or part owned in the future by the fans and the community.

It was through reports like this one that Premier League chief executive Richard Scudamore hailed the ownership model at Swansea as 'the ideal model of ownership', and we genuinely hope that maybe there will come a day when we are not looked upon as a unique model, but there will be more clubs like us as there is nothing more painful than hearing of other clubs in trouble.

Interestingly, we are contacted often by other clubs' trusts when they are looking for advice on how to run their trust, or what they can do to salvage the mess in which they find themselves. Clubs such as Newcastle, Portsmouth, Coventry, Exeter, Cardiff, Glasgow Rangers, Blackburn Rovers and Hearts have either asked for assistance and guidance in the last few years, or been highlighted as clubs that would do well to follow the Swansea model. In addition, we have been asked to present as an organisation at many meetings of trusts, including a recent meeting of Premier League trusts in Birmingham.

If we felt that our first season in the Premier League was going to be the one that saw us at our busiest, then we were not prepared for the two events that increased press coverage in the summer of 2012. Brendan Rodgers' departure to Liverpool to be replaced by Michael Laudrup and the signing of Ki Sung-Yeung sparked an interest in Swansea that had not been seen before – notably in Denmark and South Korea. That gave us new journalists to talk to and they became the latest areas where people sat up and saw the Swansea model as remarkable. It was around this time that we made the decision – probably long overdue – to try and keep records of some of the articles where we had been written about at length. The nature of the written press in particular means you cannot keep track of everything; however, I hope that the following extracts give you a good idea of some of the coverage that we have had in the last twelve months alone, and how wide-ranging the coverage can be:

South Wales Evening Post, 27 September 2012
'Swans fans in memory keepsake'

Swansea City Supporters' Trust have produced a book of fans' memories and stories to mark the club's centenary.

Packed with photographs from across the club's history, the 192-page book contains contributions from fans of all ages – from schoolchildren to those who saw their first game in the 1920s.

The stories are both funny and sad and reflect the club's colourful and sometimes turbulent history.

'It's a book about passion and commitment,' a trust spokesman said. 'It's about cheering in the stands and looking out for results on the other side of the world.

'It's about favourite spots on the terrace and strange superstitions.

'It's about family and friends. It's about why we care. It's about why we're "Swansea 'til I die".'

Herald Scotland, 21 October 2012
'Success on a shoestring'

Memories remain vivid of taking over, together with a consortium of local businessmen and the Swansea City Supporters' Trust, which has a 20 per cent share in the club and nominate a director.

Anyone buying a ticket with a credit card in those days found their account debited to Casey's Roofing – Jenkins' firm. 'We hadn't got the facilities at the club,' he said. 'We scraped around every week for money to pay the bills and keep the club going.'

Then, the club's annual turnover was £1.7 million. Last season it was £65 million, including a healthy profit. Swansea spent more money on transfers in the summer of 2011 than in their previous ninety-nine years of history.

The Express, 15 November 2012
'Portsmouth administrator signs deal for fans to buy club'

Supporters' trusts have taken over a growing number of clubs in England but most so far have been in the lower leagues, although Premier League Swansea City are part-owned by their trust. Elsewhere, it is more common. Most top German teams are majority or wholly owned by their fans, as are Barcelona. In the United States, the Green Bay Packers NFL team are 100 per cent fan owned.

Ashley Brown, chairman of the Pompey Supporters' Trust said, 'We are thrilled and proud to have signed a sale agreement with the administrator to buy and run Portsmouth Football Club. We hope to finalise the sale by Christmas, and go into 2013 with a fresh start for our great club.

'This is a special day for the thousands of Pompey fans who have stood by their club and stood up to be counted.'

South Wales Evening Post, 8 November 2012
'Swans are in Europe'

Members of the Swansea City Supporters' Trust paid a visit to the European Parliament in Brussels to join an event organised by

Supporters Direct Europe, to launch a report on how supporter involvement through team membership can improve the game.

They met with MEP Jill Evans who said 'Swansea supporters' trust has a 20 per cent shareholding in Wales only Premier League club, and is seen by Supporters Direct Europe as something of a flagship trust. It is unique among the multi-millionaire owned Premier League clubs.'

The Guardian, 8 January 2013
'The "different route" that lifted Swansea from doldrums to delirium'

Jenkins ascribes the loss-making financial whirlpool as the reason so many clubs are sold to overseas investors, including Cardiff City, now owned by Malaysians, while Swansea are owned by local people, and 20 per cent by the supporters' trust, the envy of fans at many other clubs. 'We all take pride in going against the norm, where clubs lose millions of pounds and need owners to pump money in,' Jenkins says. 'There is no need for it.'

Huw Cooze, elected by the supporters' trust to serve as its director on the club's board, says that, with hindsight, the circumstances favoured the trust, allowing it to buy such a significant stake when the club was facing collapse. 'It has worked out well for us, and it keeps the club close to the supporters; we feel it is still our club,' Cooze says. 'Ten years ago we were down with the dead men, nearly out of the league. Now we hope Michael Laudrup can take us to another level. The feel-good factor in Swansea is huge, and yes, we are all proud of our club.'

Football Courier, 29 January 2013
'6 Things Swansea City Are Doing Right'

When Swansea nearly dropped out of the Football League ten years ago, the Swansea City Supporters Society Ltd was set up in order to maintain the interest of the supporters within the club.

In truth, it was mainly set up to ensure that there would still be a club, such was the level of turmoil at the time.

Ten years on, the same trust still has a 20 per cent holding in the Welsh club, as well as an elected member who sits on the board of directors. All Swansea season ticket holders are permitted to join the trust upon purchase of their ticket.

In an age where big-wigs and suits make the majority of decisions in regards to the running of Premier League clubs, it is refreshing to see a set-up where the opinions of the fans are seriously taken on board.

While it is common across Europe, there are not enough cases in the Premier League where fans have a say in all day-to-day club issues.

Again, Swansea are setting another trend that others should follow.

Supporters Direct Press Release, January 2013 'Supporters Direct backs culture and sport committee's findings'

David Lampitt said, 'The positive role that supporters can play is no better demonstrated than by looking at the success of Swansea City, FC United of Manchester or the Bundesliga in Germany. Fans are not the cause of the game's problems, but they can be, they must be, part of the solution. SD will continue to push for these reforms working alongside our partner organisations, the football authorities and the Government.'

BBC Sport Online, 17 January 2013

There is no doubt that fan-ownership, as a business model, is an idea whose time has come.

For years, the prevailing view among football's ruling classes was that the only clubs fans could run were 'phoenix clubs', effectively the souls of the deceased teams, starting again in the outer reaches of the non-League galaxy.

The thought of fans in boardrooms, and owners in the stands, was dismissed as unworkable, and arguments that it seems to work OK for Barcelona, Real Madrid and most of the Bundesliga were usually met with talk of different starting points and footballing traditions.

Perceived failures of fan-ownership at clubs like Brentford, Chesterfield, Notts County, Stockport County and York City did not help in shifting this idea, although Supporters Direct spokesman Kevin Rye sees these ownerships as successes.

'There's a particularly lazy lie that still gets peddled by some: that supporters' trusts like those at Brentford, Chesterfield or York City were failures,' he said. 'These were in fact outstanding successes for the fans in not just keeping them alive, but ensuring that they could have futures beyond the daily grind of just survival. The only failure was of football regulation to address the impact of an un-level playing field created by unsustainable spending, and our job still hasn't finished.'

As recently as two years ago, the only fan-owned club in the Football League was Exeter City. But the last two seasons have seen that number swell to three – AFC Wimbledon completing their remarkable journey from the outer reaches, and Wycombe Wanderers being saved by their fans – with Pompey trying to make it four and Wrexham top of the Blue Square Bet Premier.

It is also worth noting that fans of media darlings Swansea City have a 20 per cent stake in their club.

BBC Sport Online, 22 February 2013
'Capital One Cup Final: Swans fans at heart of club's success'

'I'm involved in everything,' said Huw Cooze. 'I'm asked an opinion on everything. It's like any board of any company and it's run democratically. It's as simple as it can be.

'I've fought hard for certain issues for supporters and I've won some and I've lost some. I accept that I can't win them all.

'I've got people out there who are listening and watching websites – I do it myself, I know Huw (Jenkins) does and I know the others do. We're supporters. We know what supporters want but can't always give it.'

He added, 'I would say it's 100 per cent the way forward and it's good to have a supporter who's fighting their corner but it's quite important as well to have the rest of the board who are supporters.'

Sporting Life, 19 February 2013
'Jenkins is Swansea's driving force'

Alan Lewis said, 'We have had contact with dozens of other supporters' trusts, but obviously we had a very specific set of circumstances at the time we were formed.

'There is no checklist you can follow as those dire circumstances in 2001 were what gave us the opportunity to get involved.

'But, if we are held up as an example to others then that is great. As a trust and a club we never imagined we would be where we are and obviously if it can happen here, then why can't it happen for other clubs?'

South Wales Evening Post, 11 April 2013
'Swansea City Supporters' Trust delighted to receive dividend following record club profits'

The trust, which has more than 13,000 members, received £199,999 from a £1 million dividend, which reflected its 19.99 per cent share holding in the club.

Trust chairman Phil Sumbler said, 'The accounts confirm the prudent nature in which we operate, and the current board are to be commended for their careful management within budgets, while also allowing us to remain competitive on the field.

'In terms of the interim dividend, the trust board fully backed the vote of the directors.'

This is, of course, just a flavour of the coverage that we have had over the past twelve months and does not take into account appearances on the radio, television or other media outlets. What it does show is that the work we have done here at Swansea is seen as hugely positive and a definite model that other clubs should be looking to follow.

It would be remiss of me not to look back in this chapter at one particular media exchange back in 2006 not long after the club had moved to the Liberty Stadium. One of the issues that the trust had always talked around at the time was the need for the club to have a chief executive. It was a widespread view of the fans at the time and it was believed that the club needed to make this change to progress.

In an exchange earlier in 2006, the trust were supporting publicly a need for that chief executive, which was being backed vocally by fans on the various Internet sites. However, in the only really public exchange between club and trust in recent years this was a claim dismissed by the club chairman via *Wales on Sunday*.

He insisted that the appointment would be a waste of money:

> Frankly, I think these people are talking utter garbage. It's a ludicrous suggestion to make.
>
> There's no need for a chief executive at Swansea. The club is unique in that we're not responsible for the running of the stadium or the day-to-day running of matches.
>
> Stadco are fully responsible for those things – 99 per cent of football clubs do have to run those things which is the reason they've got a chief executive. But why would we need one? It makes no sense.
>
> Perhaps people think we should have one because Cardiff have got one. I don't know, but it won't be happening. We're not going to pay money out that would be a lot better spent on the playing side.
>
> We're set up to provide funds for players' wages not for administration. That's why we've been successful over the past couple of years. All clubs should be geared that way.
>
> A chief executive takes wages out of a club but he has no control at all. He's just a puppet of the board.

It should be noted as well that in the AGM minutes of the trust from 2006 there was a question raised regarding the off-field administration at the club, and the need for a chief executive to run the club on a day-to-day basis. The trust board had on previous occasions raised the subject with the club board but it had been rebuffed on each occasion with the chairman particularly vocal against the proposal. At the 2006 AGM it was agreed that the trust continue to encourage the appointment of a CEO, a motion that was carried unanimously. However, as time has gone on we have let go of the argument for the reasons outlined by the chairman in the article referred to above. And, in fairness, since his appointment to a full-time role at the club he has possibly carried out that role to a greater degree than any appointment we could have made, particularly when we know that the board would not give any external appointee the autonomy that they would need.

So media-wise it has been an interesting time for us since our formation, and thanks to a great team of people, over the years we have featured in what I believe to be thousands of media appearances that have promoted the name of Swansea City Supporters' Trust worldwide and given us recognition for what we are – a flagship model for supporters' trusts everywhere.

15

The Future

Again, you can't connect the dots looking forward; you can only connect them looking backwards. So you have to trust that the dots will somehow connect in your future. You have to trust in something – your gut, destiny, life, karma, whatever. This approach has never let me down, and it has made all the difference in my life.

Steve Jobs, 1955–2011

So what of the future? I think it is safe to say that if I had asked that question back in the summer of 2001, there is no way that I would have predicted what was to happen in a ten-year period. The Premier League was a dream and there was almost an acceptance in football that the top flight was the province of the elite clubs that had an almost bottomless pit of money. Foreign investors in football clubs were led by Roman Abramovich with his takeover of Chelsea and for a club like us it was a million miles away from where we could even dream to be, let alone actually live that dream.

But what you have seen in this book is that we had belief and through hard work, dedication and a whole dollop of luck then we rewrote football business models almost single-handed and proved that it is possible. And because of this, it would be crazy to predict where we may be as an organisation in say two, five or even ten years' time. However, we have to be prepared for many possibilities and our place in the Premier League makes one of those possibilities more likely. It is one that we have discussed time and time again as a trust board, and that is the question of what we would do if an outside investor came in and wanted to sink money into the football club. How would we as an organisation react and what would be our answer if we were ever asked the question?

As a gut reaction I would almost instantly say that we would not sell. My mind always goes back to Notts County Supporters' Trust, who gave up their ownership of the club in 2009 on the back of new investment. Alarmingly, their trust did not sell their 60 per cent stake; they gifted it to the new owner and did not safeguard their position on the board going forward. At the time, Dave Boyle, who advised us so greatly, was extremely critical of the decision and his words always ring loud and clear when I think about it. Dave said,

> We believe that it was not right for Notts County that the trust gave its shares away to unnamed investors without securing a continuing role for supporters in decision making.
>
> The principles behind supporters' trusts are that football clubs are community institutions that depend on fans' loyalty, and that clubs will benefit from fans owning shares and being represented on the board. The Notts County Supporters' Trust's own objectives were to seek ownership in the club, which it had, and representation in its running, which it also had, so by giving those away, the trust went against its very reasons for existing.

A former trust board member, David Hindley, also added,

> Supporters worked extremely hard to secure the future of the club when it was faced with possible liquidation and the trust was committed to openness. Yet still we do not even know who our new owners are, important details like the source of the money have not been made public, and the trust has not retained any shares or representation in the club. That is not what the trust stood for.

When you look back at the events at Notts County in the four years since the trust gave up their shares, you have a club still not progressing and the representation that they worked hard to achieve no longer in place. I think it is safe to say that we would not want to lose our twelve years' hard work without safeguards for the trust, so the initial reaction would always be not to sell. From our point of view, the shareholding of the club is split between seven different shareholders and that in itself provides a safeguard in that any potential outside investor needs to persuade several shareholders to sell to be able to gain control. We must also remember that there is a caveat in the shareholders' agreement that any sale of shares must be offered to existing shareholders first before outside investors can be considered.

Of course, while we are in the Premier League the club will always be an attractive proposition to people who, for want of a better description, do not have the same passion and commitment to the club as the current investors. Conservatively, you may estimate that the current value of the club is upwards of £50 million and therefore fifty times the original valuation. If that valuation is reasonable then the smallest investor at 5 per cent would see the value of their shares at £2.5 million and that has to be a windfall attraction to them should it ever happen. So what would we do if that potential investor comes forward and makes a bid for the club?

The first thing to make clear is that we cannot make that decision alone as a trust board. We can meet, dissect any potential offer and make a recommendation, but that has to go in front of our voting members as to what they want us to do with the offer. Simply, if the voting members said sell, we would have to sell. Interestingly here, because of our shareholding at 21 per cent of the club, we find ourselves in a position that any rejection from us (or the other two largest shareholders) makes any investment less attractive to these potential investors. An investment into 79 per cent of the club would never be as appealing to an outsider, despite the fact that they would still be the majority shareholder and could effectively make the decisions they wanted, but they would have to do it with us in their ear passing on the views of the fans, and being able to communicate with the fans any decision that we felt was going to be unpopular or inappropriate. Put it this way: it would be like having advance notice that Tony Petty was about to sack the players rather than reacting to it after the event.

Inevitably, taking any potential offer to the members opens up the possibility that we could lose our shareholding no matter how much as a board we would want to hold onto it. Imagine your view if a potential new owner came on board with a war chest that approached a quarter of a billion pounds for team strengthening. We have seen what that has done at Manchester City and we appreciate that it looks and sounds attractive. Some may take the view that blocking the offer may make us unpopular and we could be mandated to sell by our members. In such a situation I think the only thing that we could do, if instructed by members to do so, is sell. However, we would need, if that was the case, to learn from the mistakes of Notts County and put in the safeguards that ensure all our hard work is not wasted. That may necessitate the ability to buy back our shares at no more than what we had sold them for – possibly less if we played in a lower division. It may be that we write into any deal that we retain a seat on the board after the sale, to preserve that input into club affairs, or there could be other safeguards in place. But we have to think of our history, where we have come from, and ensure that we retain that aim of maintaining a professional club in Swansea. All too often we have seen clubs fall from grace after a period of bad management, and in our position we should be able to ensure that it never happens to Swansea again.

At the current time all of this is hypothetical, as there are no investors in the background, and if I was being honest I do not believe that we need them as the club has ticked along nicely, growing steadily through the correct management. We have no way of knowing how people would react to any offers – either our membership or other shareholders – so all we can say on this front is we will react if and when we have to rather than making predictions.

Of course, there is the possibility that at some stage the football circle can go full turn and we could find ourselves back in the lower divisions of the Football League. While this is something that none of us would wish to happen, the retaining of our dividends as a 'rainy day' fund is something that we would consider to be important, as it allows us to assist if at some stage in the future the club needs it. In the Premier League our current war chest of £400,000 is not a large sum, but it would be in the lower divisions, and that is something that we must always bear in mind.

Money is a massive part of football these days and it is scary, when you look at the turnover of the football club now with the money received from the Premier League TV deals, and of course a much larger commercial presence than we have ever experienced before. It is difficult to imagine any form of financial pressure hitting the club, especially given the prudent way that it is managed, but with multi-million-pound turnover comes multi-million-pound expenditure, and there is always the possibility of a bad business decision causing financial problems in the future. It is therefore somewhat pleasing to see politicians lobbying for fans to have an automatic right to take over football clubs hit by financial crisis.

The proposals suggest that fans be given six months' grace to take over any club that enters administration. Better still, if the fans succeed then they avoid a points deduction, which is a great incentive as it has always seemed a little unfair that a team heading into administration is given such deduction, which normally would lead to relegation, thus intensifying the problem. The proposal also suggests that a 'right to observe' would be established to allow a representative from a football supporters' trust to attend club board meetings. While this is not an issue for us at Swansea right now, it is encouraging to see that there are people looking to increase influence at other clubs in trouble. As Labour MP for Harrow West, Gareth Thomas comments, 'Fans are the foundation of every successful football club and deserve a greater say in how their club is run.'

These proposals are at an early stage but it will be a great step forward if they come to fruition and certainly something that we at Swansea would wholeheartedly support.

And it is not just in this country that people seem to be waking up and backing supporter ownership of football clubs. At this year's European Football Fans' Congress in Amsterdam, UEFA General Secretary Gianni Infantino declared,

Supporters investing in a club can only be good for the game. At a time when the global crisis and the lack of financial discipline are threatening the very survival of many football clubs, supporter involvement offers a credible, sustainable alternative to the current model of club ownership and governance.

While players, coaches and even owners change with increasing frequency, supporters remain loyal to the colours they proudly wear. And because fans are the reason football exists at all, your voice has to be heard and fans have to help shape football's future. UEFA is proud to have established a dialogue with your representatives that allows us to share with you our thoughts and proposals but also lets us pick your brains, get your ideas, answer your complaints and evaluate your suggestions.

All of this is a far cry from our formation, when trusts found they were treated with suspicion by many, and it was widely said that supporter ownership in football could not be sustained and was not a business model that would work. There are still people that retain that belief, but we believe that our work has shown that it is possible to have a successful model incorporating supporter ownership and our views as an organisation continue to be heard at some of the highest levels.

Overall, in terms of our shareholding of the football club, I do not envisage this changing in the future, but I am sure that as you see here we are thinking broadly in terms of what could happen, and ensuring that we are never caught unawares if the unexpected happens. The big part for us, though, is that the club board and other shareholders see the value in us as an organisation and that gives us a further level of protection that is not always afforded to trusts at other clubs.

Outside of the shareholding and input into the football club, the future holds for us a further expansion of the work that we have done to bring the club closer to the community. Since the payment of the two dividend payments we have started talking to junior football leagues about working in partnership with them with some level of sponsorship. Although we have nothing concrete on this front at the moment, we believe that something along these lines will encourage young supporters to go on and become Swans supporters for life. I know when I look back at our glory years of the late 1970s and early 1980s as a youngster, the success then hooked me into the football club and that passion has never subsided. If we can do something similar with the youth leagues in and around the Swansea catchment area then that could inspire a future generation of Swans fans and that is important to us. It is not just the leagues in Swansea we are talking to; we are looking at leagues east and west of Swansea and also talking through with Macron, who currently support these leagues, to see if we can work together for the benefit of junior football.

Our social calendar also remains full. The annual bowling night will continue, as will the awards dinner, and we certainly never want to see an end to the fans' forums, which always prove popular. In a perfect world I think we would see a day where we take forums back on the road, but to do so – more so these days where pressure is greater on the time of the players and management – we need to be convinced that we can get a large turnout to justify events outside of Swansea. However, we also have to be mindful of the spreading word of Swansea City, and ensure that all supporters feel close to their club, not just those that live within the boundaries of an SA postcode.

Recently, representatives from the Swans Trust have been asked to address meetings of both Premier League trusts and the national Supporters Direct conference, and this is something that I would like to see us develop further. We have seen constantly through this book that we have a business model that is envied by others who would like to replicate it, and that is why we should push our message as often as we can do. Circumstances dictate that we may not have as much time as we would like to spread this word, but when we are able to, it is hugely satisfying as not only does it show us in a good light as a trust, but also improves the image of the football club because fans realise that the two organisations are working completely hand in hand. Add to that the opportunities that we get when other trusts come forward and ask for advice and there is definitely more that we would like to do on this front.

We are twelve years into our history and I do not think it is possible to even try and predict where we may be in another twelve years' time. There have been points in that period where we may have believed that the club could go no further, but they keep proving that theory wrong. All we can do is continue on the route that we have taken during our history, and that is to retain a close working relationship with the club and maintain the work that we have done outside of that, which is afforded to us by our presence as a shareholder and board member of the club. If the next twelve years are anywhere near as good as the first twelve then I do not think any of us would offer up even the gentlest complaint.

Conclusion

The story of Swansea City Supporters' Trust and Swansea City Football Club over the past eleven or so years is nothing short of incredible. You may take that as a biased view, and maybe it is, but as someone who was there in the heat of battle playing my own little part, right through to the head of the organisation that owns more than one fifth of a Premier League football team, it just seems incredible that we can have helped transform a club that was dying on its feet to one of the leading clubs in the English football pyramid.

It is completely mad to think that the actions of one man galvanised the club in the way that it did. When Tony Petty first engaged in talks with Mike Lewis over the purchase of Swansea City, I do not suspect he had any idea of what he was entering into, nor what reaction his actions would arouse in a group of football supporters that, for many years, had sat back and watched the mismanagement of their football club. His time at the club was incredible to watch, and to see so many people from different walks of life join forces to remove him from the club was remarkable. While some just caused untold chaos through written words, protests at games and some small annoying tactics, in among it all were people who were preparing the business plan to ensure that the club had a future. Make no mistake – had it not been for all these things we may not have ground Petty down. It was the actions and words that he eventually grew tired of, and the presence of the trust and the consortium was the only place he could turn to as his outlet for selling the football club; a perfect team effort that many should follow and an example that football fans do have a choice and do not just have to accept that what is put in front of them is what they have to deal with.

From there it has been another team effort to lift the club to where they are now, a team effort during which we have more than played our part. The club have turned to us when they have needed supporters galvanised, whether it be through a fundraising event or just to help drag more people through the gates. Family days, open days, fans' forums and social nights have all made this a pretty unique football club at this level, and from my point of view being involved is great fun and hugely satisfying.

With much hard work also comes a few strokes of luck, and as a club we have taken some gambles over that period whether it be a player purchase, managerial appointment or general business decision, but in the main they have worked and three promotions, a new stadium and many tens of millions of pounds will tell you that we have got it right, not just as a club but as a trust as well.

At times during our own journey we have been criticised, and rightly so at times. As an organisation we cannot always pretend we are going to get it right, but I do like to think that we listen and will take up the fight when we can and improve things that we can do. The pinch point at the Liberty Stadium, and the issues we had around standing at the stadium, are just two examples of things we managed to change; there are still more and we continue to raise issues, whatever they may be. The phrase 'matchday experience' may be a new one that has been used more and more in recent years, but while it exists we are committed to making it as enjoyable as possible for as many supporters as is feasible.

If you go back to the very early days of the trust then I do not think we ever believed that we would own a share of the club, let alone a share that could be valued at £10 million or more. But such was the way that everyone backed the football club back in 2001 that this became possible and we grew in size as an organisation alongside the football club itself.

In this book we have tried to tell the story of the club's rise from our own perspective and hopefully given you an insight into what part we played in the original battle to win back the football club, and also our activities as an organisation since then. There have been many thousands of hours poured into trust activities, be they meetings, organisation of events, club activities or our favourite task, envelope stuffing, but each of those hours has been worth it and I hope have improved the way that fans feel about Swansea City. As a fan for over thirty-five years, I know what this club means to me and therefore it will mean the same to many others, so it is always worth the hard labour when a plan comes to fruition.

Two names cropped up in this book on many occasions as absent friends for the trust and before we close I would like to mention them both again. Richard Lillicrap was a driving force behind the Swans Trust. His articulate view, unique sense of humour and passion for the supporters' trust movement in total led to many of our long-term trust members being supporters of our organisation in the first place. His work as our representative with Supporters Direct eventually led to him being elected to the Supporters Direct board and it was a sad, sad day when I learned of his death.

Likewise, Mike Kent was a huge supporter of ours. Mike actually believed that we should aim for 100 per cent trust ownership and passionately used to explain his logic behind that. He stood at the first meeting of the trust and again his words inspired others and he played a huge part in us forming a trust in the first place.

Both Richard and Mike would have a huge amount of pride at the coverage that we now get as an organisation – they always believed we could be a role model for others to follow and now that we are there is a very large chunk of that which is down to them. Sadly, neither of them saw our rise into the Premier League, but like so many Jacks who have passed before and after them they now have some of the best seats in the house to watch our brand of football and our success. Thanks guys, we simply could not have done it without you.

I hope you have enjoyed this book and I hope that we have done the journey justice. I know that there is more to come from the Swansea City story and as the club continues to grow and progress then we will continue to move with it as one of the premier supporters' trusts of all time. Be proud of whatever part you have played in that.

Here's to more success in the future.

Acknowledgements

It is traditional in books like these to thank the people who made it possible. In twelve years, so many people have helped Swansea City Supporters' Trust that it is almost impossible to thank everyone individually, so we apologise to anyone who we haven't named but there are so many people that we would need to write another book just to accommodate you!

Our first thanks, therefore, go to the endless volunteers that we have had over the years, either as fundraisers, raffle ticket sellers, helpers at social events, people who held buckets at bucket collections, our regular and one-off donators of funds and the thousands of people who have turned up at our social gatherings and forums to show their support for the both the club and the trust.

On top of these we would like to thank the following people:

Huw Jenkins and Kevin Johns MBE for their continued support and kind words in the forewords of this book.

Steve McLelland, John Gregory and Ray Trotman at the executive fundraising committee for their assistance at our social events.

Our four trust chairmen, John Parkhouse, Leigh Dineen, Ron Knuszka and Phil Sumbler, for leading from the front.

Our two supporter directors, Leigh Dineen and Huw Cooze, for their work on the club board and representing the views of the supporters.

Will Morris, Nigel Hamer, Cath Dyer and Huw Cooze for the photographs included in this book.

Dave Boyle, formerly of Supporters Direct, for his many hours in Swansea during the set-up of the trust.

Our friends at Supporters Direct for their continued support and guidance and for representing the views of supporters' trusts everywhere.

To Huw Jenkins, Leigh Dineen, Huw Cooze, Gwilym Joseph, Brian Katzen, Don Keefe, Martin Morgan, Steve Penny, John Van Zweden, David Morgan, Will Morris and everyone behind the scenes at Swansea City Football Club. It was a thankless task in the early days but the long journey has been worth it!

Alun Cowie and all the backroom staff at Swansea City Football Club for their assistance in everything that we do.

Andrew Davies and all members of the Swansea Stadium Management Committee for their assistance in placement of the history features we have added to the Liberty Stadium.

All other people who have been involved in the setting up and running of social events and fans' forums.

Every single person who has taken the time to join the trust, whether currently or in the past. The stronger the membership, the stronger the organisation.

Richard Lillicrap, Mike Kent and every 'Internet warrior' for having the vision to make a trust possible and driving the early stages of the organisation.

The *South Wales Evening Post*, Swansea Sound and the *Western Mail* for their continued support of the trust.

Gavin Wilding at fansnetwork.co.uk for access to the jackarmy.net archive.

All the various people that have contributed to this book with their views and memories of times gone by.

Esme Allchurch, Karen and Luke James, Tudor Evans, Huw Bowen, Phil Bethell and Martin Johnes for their assistance in some of our history projects.

The management and players of Swansea City for their continued support of our social events and their honesty in answering questions at our fans' forums.

In particular, Viv Brooks, Stuart McDonald, Debbie and Brian Rees and Alan Lewis for their endless hours 'walking the beat' on matchdays to spread the trust word.

To those trust board members who have publicised us via the media over the years: Marilyn Croft, Cath Dyer, Paul Morris, Phil Sumbler, Jim White, Huw Cooze and Alan Lewis.

Jim White for the use of his customer database and Huw Cooze for the design and compilation of our annual newsletter.

And anyone else that we have forgotten.

You can contact the Swansea City Supporters' Trust by writing to us at:

12 Dynevor Avenue
Neath
SA10 7AG

Or contact us on 07977 382328 or phil@planetswans.co.uk.

About the Author

Phil Sumbler has been a Swans fan for over thirty-five years and has seen all the highs and lows of that period. As the site owner of jackarmy.net back in 2001, the site was often at the fore of breaking news from the Vetch Field and the site, among others, played its own part in the removal of Tony Petty from power at Swansea.

In 2005, he joined the board of Swansea City Supporters' Trust and a year later was appointed chairman, a position he still holds to this date.

He has previously worked with his good friend Keith Haynes on four books – *Vetch Field Voices, 100 Swansea Greats, Another Day at the Office: The Roger Freestone Story* and *The Tony Ford Story.* He has also written for many football publications, newspapers and fanzines over the years.

He is still site owner of www.planetswans.co.uk, which took over from jackarmy.net back in 2007 and is one of the most popular Swansea websites for people to keep track on the latest news and views of the Swans.

He lives just outside of Swansea with his wife Angela and daughters Lucy and Gemma, and is a long-term season ticket holder in the East Stand at the Liberty Stadium.

You can contact Phil by emailing him at phil@planetswans.co.uk.

Join the Supporters' Trust

For the 2013/14 season the trust is offering two levels of membership:

e-Membership will be free of charge but does not give voting rights, You will receive our annual newsletter and regular e-newsletters. All members from the 2012/13 season will have automatically become e-members for the 2013/14 season, and so if you were a member last season, and wish to continue as an e-member only, you don't need to do anything. We will already have all of your membership details on our database.

Standard Membership will require payment of a membership fee. You will receive newsletters as for e-members, be able to take part when members are asked to vote on certain issues, e.g. trust elections (excludes Junior members), and stand for election to the trust board (if over eighteen).

To find more about joining the Swansea City Supporters' Trust, please contact info@swanstrust.co.uk or call 07977 382328.

Our Website

You can visit the Swans Trust website at www.swanstrust.co.uk or follow us on Twitter @SwansTrust.

Our website contains all the latest minutes from our board meetings and, if you would like to see these, then please log on monthly to have a read. You will also find details of our latest upcoming events and further information about the trust and our previous events.

You can also support the trust with regular donations or by using the two simple schemes below:

Easyfundraising

Easyfundraising is a shopping directory listing some of your favourite online stores, including Amazon, Next, Debenhams, John Lewis, Toys 'R' Us, HMV and over 500 other top-name stores. Whenever you shop with any one of them using the links provided on the easyfundraising site, you'll generate a free donation for us of up to 15% of the purchase price every time! It really is that simple!

It doesn't cost a penny more to shop and raise funds in this way. In fact you can even save money, as many retailers give exclusive discounts, special offers and even 'e-vouchers' when you shop through the easyfundraising site.

All you need to do is register free at http://www.easyfundraising. org.uk/swanseacity and use easyfundraising every time you shop online.

So register now – what are you waiting for?

Register today at www.easyfundraising.org.uk/swanseacity and help us to raise funds. Every penny you raise will help us continue our vital work.

Easysearch

You can also raise funds for us every time you search the Web, with easysearch, a search engine with a difference!

When you search with easysearch, you'll raise around 1p for us with every search you make! Make just ten searches a day and you could raise £25 a year – or more – for us, just by switching to easysearch.

What's more, easysearch combines the strengths of several search engines together – Yahoo!, MSN Live Search, Ask.com and many more – making it a 'super' search engine! Easysearch tracks down the most relevant and accurate results from across the Web, which means you'll find what you are looking for quickly and easily every time - in one 'easy' search.

Please set our unique easysearch page, http://swanseacity. easysearch.org.uk, as your homepage and use it every time you search the Web.